Book Cover by James Chakhtoura
ISBN# 979-8-9894451-0-3

I0459353

THANK YOU

Thank you, Thomas Strunk, for being such a positive inspiration and influence in my life. You have directly helped change my life for the better by inspiring me to adjust my mindset and attitude. You are the catalyst for my motivation, responsible for directing me to spend my time sharing the things I have learned in my journey so that it may help others along their way.

I also want to thank my parents, grandparents, and all of my family, friends, business partners, and other associates who have had a positive, impactful, and monumental influence in my life.

In addition, I'd like to thank Nicolas A. Houpt, Jeffrey James Meredith, Jr., as well as Coach Corey Wayne, as I would not be the man I am today without them.

–Justin M. Bullock

I'd like to thank my family and friends for supporting me in this endeavor of becoming an author and bringing this book to fruition. To all of the people who've helped make this possible with the encouragement and guidance they've offered and to all who have pre-ordered this book, I thank you all from the bottom of my heart.

This book is dedicated to my uncle Tommy Houpt, whose life was taken far too soon. In the short time he was here, he was able to brighten the lives of everyone he met and knew. He taught me to listen without interruption, to truly hear, understand, weigh my options before making any major decisions, and, most importantly, to be humble in all that I do.

When pride comes, then comes disgrace, but with humility comes wisdom.
–Proverbs 11:2

You will be greatly missed.

–Nicolas A. Houpt

OUR MISSION & VISION

Tilting The Balance™ is a transformative system designed to help individuals cultivate balance, purpose, and fulfillment in every area of life. The origin of this framework traces back to December 26th, 2019, when Justin experienced a moment of absolute clarity while sitting in his mother's driveway, just before leaving to visit his grandparents. Every hair on his body stood up as an undeniable realization hit him

Despite consuming countless personal and professional development books and content alongside his close friend Nicolas Houpt, they both remained stuck. Nothing seemed to be working to help them overcome their cycles of acquiring knowledge without attaining significant results. At that moment, Justin called Nick with a proposal:

"Nick! Let's commit to a thirty-day challenge together, hold each other accountable, and write a book about our experiences!" What if Nick would not have answered that call, in more ways than one? That single conversation sparked what they never could have initially imagined would evolve into what it became over the course of nearly six years.

Through rigorous testing, refinement, and real-world application over that time, Justin and Nick transformed their initial thirty-day experiment into a proven framework. What began as two friends trying to break free from their own limiting patterns and beliefs developed into a complete, practical methodology that has helped countless individuals create lasting transformation. In the process, they discovered something profound. Most people are not starving for more information. They are overwhelmed by it. Never in human history have people had more access to information. There are more books, podcasts, videos, courses, and educational streams of advice available than one person could spend an entire lifetime consuming. Yet individuals today struggle to apply what they learn more than ever before. How is this possible?

Around every corner are free newsletters, posts, or videos, accompanied by advertisements selling strategies to get rich quick, lose weight without effort, or instantaneously turn from failure to success. Even when programs are built with integrity, genuine does not always mean effective, and effective does not always mean comprehensive. A program can work within its narrow focus but still fail to help someone integrate that growth into the rest of their life. Think of life like a master puzzle where purpose forms the complete image, but within that larger picture are smaller, distinct sections representing relationships, health, career, finances, and other aspects of existence and personal growth. Most people try to work on these areas independently, treating each as an isolated challenge. Real progress is not about excelling in one area while neglecting others. *Tilting The Balance*™ reveals how all the scattered pieces from different areas of life fit together within the bigger picture of purpose. It is about knowing how to implement insights in balance so that each piece connects together and strengthens the whole. Growth in one area should support, rather than disrupt, the entirety of well-being.

This discovery revealed a critical gap in personal development. Despite years of consuming countless resources, Justin and Nick remained stuck because no method existed to teach them how to strategically apply everything they were learning. Born out of their mutual frustration, what makes *Tilting The Balance*™ unique is that it addresses this execution gap that many traditional resources overlook. While these tend to focus solely on either motivation, mindset, or teaching practical strategies on specific subjects, this framework provides what often remains the missing piece. It offers a clear methodology that helps individuals compartmentalize their thoughts, define their purpose, organize their priorities, and execute with precision, in that specific order.

By guiding others through *"The 10 Categories of Life," "The 10 Fundamentals of Self-Love,"* and their built-in accountability with *"The 3-4-30 Challenge*SM*,"* paired with proven exercises and a comprehensive step-by-step approach, individuals seeking meaningful change can finally gain the structure needed to turn knowledge into lasting results. This formulaic approach helps determine what to learn, why it matters, how it serves growth, when to learn it, where to best focus efforts, and who to learn from. Rather than mindlessly consuming content, it provides strategic clarity on exactly what knowledge is needed and how to implement it most effectively.

As the authors, our mission is to empower one billion people to believe in themselves, practice ongoing disciplined action, and live a complete life of love, passion, purpose, and fulfillment. We understand that reaching one billion people will likely extend far beyond our own lifetimes, and we welcome that challenge. Whether it takes generations or centuries, we envision *Tilting The Balance*™ outlasting us. We want it to become a foundational resource in both personal and professional development, the first guide that people turn to when they decide they are ready to transform their lives and circumstances.

Our objective is not about the number of individuals who directly read our material or engage with our programs. If we can influence one person to use this system to launch something that revolutionizes the world, one person to treat others more positively, or another to inspire growth in their community, then each of those leads to compounding contributions toward the billion lives we aim to reach. The more someone improves their relationship with themselves, the stronger family member, friend, partner, professional, and person they can become. The better someone treats others, the more compassion they may inspire in return. That influence extends far beyond people. It affects how we care for the planet, the animals and creatures we share it with, and the causes we choose to support. Each person carries responsibility to leave the world better than they found it.

This is how we measure our impact. It begins with each reader. With you. If this book creates a personal breakthrough, if you start a meaningful project, or if you change the lives of others because of what you learn here, please share it in any way possible. Tag us online, use our dedicated hashtag #TTB4E (Tilting The Balance For Everyone), or contact us directly at www.TiltingTheBalance.com/ContactUs to share your story.

What matters most to us is that transformation is happening. We see a world where people recognize their inherent value and use their gifts intentionally, without wasting their time, energy, resources, or opportunities. Too many people spend their lives without ever discovering their purpose or reaching their greatest potential. When you transform your own life and inspire others to do the same, every life improved becomes proof that our mission is alive and flourishing.

Thank you for being part of this community. We appreciate you and are beyond grateful for everyone who chooses to join us. The better we can all help people live, the better the world becomes for everyone.

Let us all work together to "tilt the balance" for the best today.

TABLE OF CONTENTS

CO-AUTHOR PROLOGUE
– Justin M. Bullock

"Success is having balance in all areas of your life."
– Brian S. Bullock

That quote from my adoptive father sparked a shift in my mindset and helped inspire the premise of this book. My name is Justin M. Bullock. A Florida native, I grew up in Tallahassee before moving to Jacksonville in November of 2013 to begin what ended up being my first professional career in the insurance industry.

My upbringing was shaped by a hardworking family. My father owned a landscaping business, while my mother worked her way up in the medical field to become a nurse and eventually medical practice administrator. Since my mother was only sixteen when she had me, both my biological father and adoptive father played significant roles in my life, with my stepfather officially adopting me at the age of five after he and my mother were married. I am forever deeply grateful for the love and guidance I received from all my parents and extended family.

Entrepreneurial influences from my grandparents on my mother's side were pivotal in shaping my values. My grandfather built a highly successful insurance company, and my grandmother ran a prosperous medical billing business. Together, they not only contributed financially but also instilled the importance of family and providing memorable experiences. My grandfather often treated our large family to trips across the U.S., covering everything from travel to accommodations. These "family gatherings" taught me the value of connection, travel, and creating opportunities for others to appreciate.

As a child, I was naturally entrepreneurial. By age seven, I was washing cars in the neighborhood, recruiting friends to help, and splitting the profits. In my early teens, I worked alongside my adoptive father in his landscaping business. A dedicated bodybuilder and powerlifter, he introduced me to the world of fitness, which ultimately helped me land my first official job at fifteen, racking weights at Gold's Gym. That role led to my certification as a personal trainer, and my drive for innovation kept me searching for the next opportunity. Over the years, I worked in customer service, hospitality, healthcare, construction, and numerous other industries, with each role imparting valuable lessons and principles along the way.

Shortly after moving to Jacksonville, I met my first business mentor, Thomas Strunk. He recognized my potential and helped me shift my mindset, encouraging me to view the world and act in entirely new ways. He also taught me that success is not just about money but more about purpose and impact. His guidance led me to real estate and online business, and his influence was instrumental in shaping my business endeavors and ultimately bringing this book and my coaching practice to life.

Another defining moment came in 2015 when my friend Jeff Meredith transformed his life after reading *The Slight Edge* by Jeff Olson. Inspired by his example, I read the book, which became a manual for my early success and ignited a lifelong passion for reading. That single book took me from reading zero books a year to nearly one hundred over the past decade, during which I absorbed wisdom from authors like Napoleon Hill, Charles Duhigg, and Gary Keller. Their teachings directly shaped many of the principles we share in this book.

My co-author, Nick Houpt, has also been a dear friend since I initially moved to Jacksonville. We met at a networking event after I had only been in town for a month or so, and his kindness in inviting me to dinner when I was new to the city marked the beginning of our powerful friendship. Writing this book together has been an honor. Our connection has endured through various business ventures and personal challenges, and that paired with our like-mindedness and thirst for growth has made him the perfect collaborator for this project.

Over the course of four intense years of building multiple real estate and construction companies, raising several million in private capital for investment syndications and small business funding, and successfully managing several hundred collective transactions, I made a pivotal decision to change course and to close those companies. I drove myself into a state of madness and neglected every area of my existence outside of business, thinking I could always rectify my physical, mental, spiritual, and relational health after I built some mega enterprise that enabled me to become the philanthropist I so desperately aspired to be. After developing *Tilting The Balance*™, I understood how all of my experiences had shaped me to commit fully to my true calling of coaching and to teaching others about the flaws in my mentality and approach.

While I maintain my license and status as a Realtor®, and continue to serve select individuals, my primary focus has shifted to empowering others to create extraordinary lives through the very principles that transformed my own. This strategic shift from building traditional businesses to empowering others reflects my deepening commitment to making a meaningful impact through my entrepreneurial expertise and life experience.

Over the years, I have acquired numerous certifications including designations as a Master Life Coach, Master Wellness Coach, Master Mindset Coach, and Entrepreneurship & Business Coach. Paired with my own personal experiences, I bring deep expertise in life mastery, business, and wellness. I strive to assist individuals in gaining clarity, building confidence, and taking meaningful action across all areas of life. From mindset and stress management to health and well-being in both personal and professional spheres, I empower people to cultivate both inner peace and outer achievement.

I also specialize in supporting career growth, financial literacy, book writing, and real estate investing, providing structured pathways for professional advancement. For those seeking stable romantic connections, my relationship coaching offers insights on how to spark and maintain attraction, communicate effectively, and develop greater emotional intelligence that impacts all life areas. My guidance extends to establishing purpose, mastering goal setting, time management, and helping those who struggle with planning or procrastination to develop lasting commitments that keep them motivated, accountable, and taking aligned action. Whether someone needs to optimize their mindset, elevate their professional and financial life, strengthen their relationships, or enhance their overall quality of life, I am passionate about providing clarity, structure, and a proven path forward.

Outside of my professional endeavors, I enjoy a wide range of hobbies, from traveling and exploring new places and the outdoors to playing disc golf, kayaking, canoeing, and hiking. I am an avid UFC and college football fan and cherish spending time with my girlfriend, family, and friends. Music is another passion of mine, having been a lifelong musician since I began playing piano at the age of six, and it remains an integral part of my life. I co-founded Affirmation Station Music, an innovative project that transforms the music landscape by embedding science-backed affirmations into emotionally moving songs across all genres. This unique approach combines intentional language with captivating sound, creating music that uplifts, heals, and rewires the subconscious mind with empowering beliefs. I also write and perform original works under the name Woodland Drives and serve as lead singer and guitarist in a local cover band. I even have an online guitar lesson course that teaches the fundamentals called Memorize The Guitar.

One of my biggest goals after launching *Tilting The Balance*™ is to release more musical albums and more helpful books. Thank you for taking the time to read about me.

I hope you find this book to be of value and that it has a tremendous, positive impact on your life.

To Your Success,

Justin M. Bullock

CO-AUTHOR PROLOGUE
– Nicolas A. Houpt

My name is Nick Houpt, and my journey began in Pittsburgh, Pennsylvania. Since August 2010, I've called Jacksonville, Florida my home. My parents, like Justin's, were also very young when they had me. When I was born, my mother was sixteen and my father was nineteen and off in boot camp. My mother gave custody of me to my dad since he had more support than she did with the help of my grandparents. For that, I am deeply grateful. I cannot begin to imagine the sacrifice and heartbreak she endured in making that decision.

Being a city boy from Pittsburgh mostly showed me a blue-collar type of lifestyle. My dad worked in a factory making wire rope (the wires you see on bridges, pulling elevators, used on cranes, etc.), and my mom did whatever jobs she could do as a young person to get by. The old adage of "go to school so you can get a good job and make a lot of money" was instilled in me at a young age, as it likely may have been for many of you as well.

To this day, my dad still thinks he could, and should, have provided and done more to be a better father to me. His influence molded me into the man I am today, and I am forever thankful for everything he did, taught me, and still teaches me. I would not change a single thing.

My mom and I are also very close. She had set me up for a better life and was by my side helping and assisting me through the biggest struggles I've endured so far. I doubt she accurately knows or understands the impact she made and how truly grateful I am for her. Luckily for me, as I stated earlier, I also had some influence from my grandparents (who were also rather young for being grandparents). When I was young, I used to hang out in the eyeglass shop my grandfather owned and operated instead of attending childcare services. While being with him all day, I was taught all about sales, networking, small business, and entrepreneurship just by being in that environment, yet somehow never heard the word "entrepreneur." However, one thing my grandpa always said to me, and I'm sure you may have heard this before: "It's not what you know, it's who you know." That adage has helped me tremendously throughout my life and career.

I may not have known it then or had seen where any of my influences came from, but by the time I was twelve, I was an active entrepreneur. I was certainly not some child prodigy who made it big, but I did successfully sell bubble gum at school. That's right—I was raking in millions with gum! Well, maybe not millions, but for a seventh grader, I was doing pretty well.

I would stop at the corner store right by my bus stop and buy brands such as Big Red, Winter Fresh, and Juicy Fruit; the little twenty-five-cent packs (at least that's what they cost back then). I'd go to school and sell a single stick for twenty-five cents and an entire pack for a dollar. Once I started making a little money, I had my stepmother pick up bulk packs at Sam's Club so I could turn an even bigger profit. Then I started getting a bit crazy and was buying all different brands and flavors of gum. I believe that was the start of my entrepreneurial life, and I have never looked back.

At twenty-two, I launched my first "real" business in network marketing. I became heavily infatuated with personal growth and uplifting people to believe in themselves because of where and how I grew up. I understood that your mindset and habits can make an incredible change in your life and can lead you out of your current circumstances. It was from that time I had a dream of writing a book to help others.

However, what is a twenty-two-year-old with his first business and no real-life success (outside of successfully peddling chewing gum in grade school, of course) going to teach anyone? I made it my mission to learn as much as I could about business, success, finance, mindset, goals, psychology, and much more in regards to self-improvement, personal development, and overall happiness.

Fast forward to the time we completed this book and I have now owned several businesses, worked in corporate sales and marketing, become a consultant, speaker, coach, and trainer for business, marketing, sales, life, and personal success, and continue to dedicate myself to grow through reading and listening to books, articles, podcasts, seminars, and other platforms that focus on personal improvement.

I have met some amazing people along the way who have mentored and taught me more than I could have ever imagined (or afforded!). This book's purpose is to share the knowledge I've gained and, more importantly, to serve as a mentor for those who may not have one.

Together, my co-author Justin and I have faced many trials and tribulations in both our personal and business lives, yet our friendship has always remained steadfast—even when we encountered challenges with one another. The process of writing this book together has built a stronger relationship, improved our communication skills, and even helped with understanding our emotional states and character.

When Justin approached me with the idea of *Tilting The Balance*™, I loved the concept and both of us took immediate, massive action together so that we could make the idea come to fruition. It is always great to surround yourself with like-minded individuals who understand the power of the concepts we are going to cover here, and you will see that explored in further detail as you read on into the content of our works. I want to make it clear that the final product you are reading is far from that original idea. This book, as with life, has been a process worth pursuing, and I am very happy and excited for how it turned out and for the impact it can have in your life.

I hope this book leaves a lasting impression on every area of your life.

Stay Blessed,

Nick

INTRODUCTION

Welcome to *Tilting The Balance*™. After years of testing and refinement, we are excited for you to learn about this comprehensive, revolutionary system built on proven scientific research and real-world experience.

This workbook is transformational for anyone ready to embrace something new, and it is designed to help individuals achieve a higher quality of life, no matter where they are today.

So, how are you feeling in this present moment? Are you lost or overwhelmed, unsure of how to make meaningful changes? Are you craving more purpose or fulfillment? Are you struggling to balance your work and personal life or having challenges properly managing tasks? Do you feel the need to create healthier routines or feel trapped in a cycle, uncertain about where to begin?

Perhaps you feel as if you are carrying the weight of the world, constantly racing against the clock without enough time for what matters most? Or maybe, you are continually worrying about your future, fretting over the past, or wondering if you are on the right path?

Whatever your situation, you are not alone. If you have already achieved success or believe you can elevate to higher plains, the concepts and philosophies in this book will help you sharpen your focus, build greater consistency, and achieve more impactful results across all areas of your life. As the authors, the development and implementation of this system has drastically benefited our lives. We are sharing it now because we believe its power will do the exact same for you.

Through a comprehensive framework that addresses every crucial dimension of your life, from personal growth to professional success, to relationships and financial well-being, this system provides the structure needed to create positive, lasting change. Whether you are pursuing new achievements, advancing in your career, or seeking a renewed sense of purpose at any stage of life, this system empowers you to master the art of balancing, organizing, and prioritizing every aspect of your life. Regardless of your age, background, or circumstances, committing to this process will lead you to personal growth.

As you move forward, you can expect to master time management, cultivate healthier habits, and establish stronger personal boundaries. You will experience greater self-love, deeper connections with others, and more control over your time, energy, and resources. By the end of this journey, you will possess all the confidence and skills necessary to turn all of your aspirations into your reality.

It is important to note that while *Tilting The Balance*™ provides the guidance for lasting results, your success is ultimately in your hands. Many people have already transformed their lives using this system, and now the same opportunity is available to you. However, most achievements require more than just reading alone. Making progress will demand your active participation and commitment to implementing these proven strategies, and your dedication to the process will determine the magnitude of your results, or the subsequent lack thereof.

Are you ready to live the life you have always imagined? Even if you still need more direction, the time to take control is now upon you. Let *Tilting The Balance*™ guide you toward a life filled with love, purpose, and fulfillment. When you learn to master the practice of "tilting the balance" in your life, anything is possible, and we are excited to have you begin by working with us.

LET'S BEGIN

Before we begin, we want to commend you for choosing *Tilting The Balance*™. You are already taking a major step toward transforming your life and circumstances.

With any significant endeavor, success usually requires thoughtful preparation. While spontaneity has its place, meaningful achievements demand clear direction. This framework offers an innovative approach to viewing your world via key, structured categories that reveal where to focus your energies and efforts most for maximum results. By the end of this book, you will be equipped to best understand how to identify your life's purpose, how to set clear intentions and manageable goals, harness the powers of a positive mindset, and embrace the power of accountability.

To properly guide you, we have developed *"The 10 Categories of Life"* to provide unprecedented clarity, purpose, and direction.

Here are "The 10 Categories of Life":
1. The Self, Core Values, & Belief Systems
2. Personal Tasks
3. Physical Fitness & Mental Wellness
4. Hobbies, Passions, & Interests
5. Family & Friend Relationships
6. Romantic Relationships
7. Spirituality
8. Charitable Giving
9. Financial Responsibilities
10. Business & Career Objectives

These categories encompass the full spectrum of life, providing a holistic view of your priorities while ensuring no area is overlooked. They also give you a practical way to compartmentalize your life, making it easier to pinpoint what areas need urgent attention or improvement.

We usually have various, ongoing activities in our lives that occur at a range of intervals. Some are one time tasks, others are recurring and never change, and others must be continually modified as we go. Life is so much smoother though when we appreciate why we are doing what we are doing, when we know exactly what we must do, and when we understand how to best do what we need to do.

"The 10 Categories of Life" in conjunction with the exercises incorporated into this workbook are designed to serve as your personal navigation system through all of life's multidimensional complexities. Think of it akin to how modern healthcare functions in many countries today, where general physicians assess your overall health and coordinate with specialists as needed. *Tilting The Balance*™ applies these same principles, helping you uncover which areas need priority while directing you toward specific strategies that will provide solutions. Our practice is like medicine for ensuring a maintainable, flourishing, balanced life.

(Authors' Note: We would have loved to call ourselves 'life doctors,' but we are not doctors and did not want to offend anyone. We have stayed at a Holiday Inn Express though! Humor aside, take a moment to look at our book's cover and review how it celebrates Earth's remarkable harmony. From cascading waterfalls and thriving ecosystems to the interplay between land, sea, and sky, it reflects our planet's extraordinary ability to sustain life. For billions of years, Earth has maintained balance through self-regulating systems that control temperature, weather, terrain formation, and so much more. Each year, our planet cycles through seasons, recreating and reinventing itself to nurture new life and restore equilibrium. This natural rhythm serves as a powerful metaphor for our own journeys. Just as Earth maintains harmony amidst constant change, we too must cultivate balance across our physical, emotional, and spiritual dimensions. Our cover's vibrant imagery reminds us that finding balance, like nature itself, is both a challenge and a gift).

The concept of "striking a balance," which Merriam-Webster defines as 'a state in which different things occur in equal or proper amounts, or have an equal or proper amount of importance,' is fundamental to our approach.

Our bodies automatically demonstrate this principle through homeostasis—a natural equilibrium between interdependent elements (Merriam-Webster). For most living beings on this planet, their bodies regulate themselves extraordinarily well, requiring little conscious effort. Blood circulates, cells regenerate, and countless other vital functions occur without our awareness. While these internal processes happen automatically, the circumstances of our conscious lives as human beings require a much greater deal of deliberate attention.

You see, although our bodies are miraculous, we still bear the responsibility of maintaining various aspects of our physical and mental conditions. Just as we need the right balance of food, water, and oxygen to survive and thrive, our lives also demand harmony between work and rest, discipline and freedom, solitude and connection. Success entails mastering this orchestration of elements. The key lies in strategically recognizing what needs immediate focus, what can progress gradually, and what can wait. These understandings enable you to allocate your efforts wisely, strengthening priority areas while sustaining others. Through this conscious cultivation across physical, mental, emotional, and spiritual realms, you can build a foundation for lasting success and fulfillment.

When striving for success, we often encounter challenges that mirror the dynamics of automobile racing. Some moments demand sprints, requiring intense bursts of energy and focus, while others can feel more like endurance races, calling for patience, resilience, and sustained effort to reach the finish line. Push too hard or too fast, and risk losing control or, even worse, blowing your engine entirely. Like a race car overheating or spinning out, we too can face consequences from rapidly pressing ourselves beyond our limits without the proper balance. Success requires knowing when to accelerate and when to pace yourself to stay on track and achieve your goals. At the same time, just as cross-country drives can reveal breathtaking landscapes and unexpected opportunities, we must remember to embrace all of life's experiences. Life is not always a race. It is essential to cherish the processes and appreciate the adventures along the way.

(Authors' Note: Strategic timing is also a critical element of success. This principle is clearly exemplified by Michael Phelps, the most decorated Olympian in history (at the time of this publication) with 28 medals (23 gold, 3 silver, and 2 bronze). In his book No Limits: The Will to Succeed, co-authored with Alan Abrahamson, Phelps revealed how his coach Bob Bowman taught him the acronym W.I.N., standing for 'What's Important Now?' By focusing on immediate priorities, Phelps established what he calls 'microwins,' small victories that compounded over time into his historic success. The W.I.N. principle focuses on present objectives and taking action, regardless of motivation. As Phelps stated in an interview with World of Business Ideas, "...if you look at the greats in anything, in any walk of life, the greats do things when they don't always want to, and that's the separation." This is why we advocate creating to-do lists for even the simplest tasks. Tracking and completing them builds momentum and can help keep you encouraged through consistent achievement).

Referring to Phelps' achievements highlights an important truth about greatness. While not everyone will become the greatest-of-all-time in their field, each of us can strive to become the finest version of ourselves. The real measure of success is not always about being the best in the world, but about giving your best to become the most extraordinary version of **yourself.**

Now that you understand these principles, we can begin to explore how to uncover your desires and turn any dreams into achievements. The chapters ahead contain practical information combined with step-by-step workbook templates that will help you generate ideas, enhance self-awareness, and organize your objectives. The framework ahead prompts you to think about what you want most and turns your desires into actionable goals and steps. Envision each goal as a mountain waiting to be conquered.

Your first step is identifying which peaks represent your aspirations. Just as climbers carefully consider their mountains, you must determine which summits are worthwhile. Some objectives are like simple hills requiring basic preparation, while others may rival Mount Everest in risk and complexity.

Even the most accomplished Everest climbers began with smaller challenges. It can take time to work toward larger-scale initiatives. This supports why, sometimes, we must start on flat ground, progress to more demanding hills, and gradually tackle increasingly more difficult terrains. This methodical sequence builds both skill and confidence. Similarly, your push toward meaningful aspirations may often entail mastering smaller, fundamental steps first, before going all out in efforts to reach greater and lasting achievements.

This is why for our most significant goals, proper planning and adaptability are crucial. Consider that since 1922, while over 6,600 daring climbers successfully reached Everest's peak, more than 300 have perished in their attempts. This sobering statistic emphasizes why thorough preparation matters. Just as every one of those mountaineers needed to assess their oxygen supplies, the weather conditions, and their gear requirements before ascending, you also must learn how to evaluate your necessary tools, potential challenges, and contingency plans. The more ambitious your endeavors, the more essential this principle becomes. While simple tasks need minimal planning, complex achievements often benefit from experienced guidance and wisdom.

This also supports why it is so vital to have a sense of purpose in the mountains you choose to climb. Understanding why you want to climb a specific mountain is crucial, as purpose itself breeds clarity and focus, which in turn drives motivation, commitment, and discipline. When your efforts are grounded in purpose, the best directions forward become much more clear, and the strength to persevere arises naturally. This approach not only fuels disciplined effort but also leads to consistency, and consistent action over time is what drives progress and meaningful results.

(Authors' Note: One of our greatest mentors, and cherished friend, Grayson Marshall Jr., had a profound realization after undergoing heart surgery. He came to understand that purpose runs deeper than simply identifying a "why." Instead of beginning with why, he teaches that we must first determine who we want to serve and how we want to help them. By focusing on these elements first, the answers to why begin to unfold naturally. This perspective shifts the pursuit of purpose from an abstract concept to an intentional, action-driven approach.

Grayson explores this philosophy in his book, Servant Made, Not Self-Made, where he reveals how true fulfillment and success stem from serving others rather than focusing solely on personal ambition. His insight aligns directly with the principles we share throughout Tilting The Balance™. Purpose is not just a motivator; it is the foundation that makes consistent action sustainable. As you continue reading, you will find more content emphasizing the power of purpose and its role in shaping a life of fulfillment, success, and lasting impact.

The goal is not only to set objectives but to align them with a deeper mission. Keep this in mind as you move forward. Living and acting with purpose will guide you toward the results that matter most).

Note also that there are always multiple ways to reach any summit. Consider French pilot Didier Delsalle, who in 2005 landed a helicopter on Everest's peak twice in two days. While his approach was innovative, his achievement still required extensive expertise and careful preparation. His success reminds us that mastery of fundamentals, combined with creative thinking, can bring about remarkable, unexpected opportunities. Whether through methodical climbing or creative approaches, the ultimate aim should always be to reach new heights. Even with the most powerful tools, knowledge, and guidance, success only begins with the courage to start. As Les Brown powerfully reminds us:

"The graveyard is the richest place on earth, because it is here that you will find all the hopes and dreams that were never fulfilled, the books that were never written, the songs that were never sung, the inventions that were never shared, the cures that were never discovered, all because someone was too afraid to take that first step, keep with the problem, or determined to carry out their dream."

New ideas constantly emerge and evolve, but they will forever need champions willing to bring them to life. Each and every creation begins with a thought. Consider how the simplest conveniences in your daily life once existed only in someone's mind. From the basic tools of language to the most advanced technology, every innovation required someone to turn a mere idea into reality. What thoughts may lie dormant within you that could reshape your world or even benefit countless others?

"Yesterday's dreams are often tomorrow's realities." —Bruce Lee

How often have you heard someone exclaim, "Hey! That was my idea!"? The truth is, without decisive action, your thoughts may remain untapped, or someone else may bring them to life instead. While we cannot provide all the immediate answers to uncover your purpose or determine your best path forward, we offer the insights and guidance needed to help you ask the right questions and discover those answers for yourself. As you continue, we urge you to have faith in this system. It works, but only if you commit to working it first.

"A goal that is not written down is just a dream." —Fitzhugh Dodson

Get ready to embark on an exciting journey of self-discovery. Through the workbook ahead, you will identify what matters most in your life and will learn how to transform any of your aspirations into achievable goals. The insights, templates, and exercises ahead will guide you step-by-step, helping you create clear routes to personal and professional success alike. Whether your dreams are modest or monumental, you will never know what is possible until you take action.

We are honored and excited for you to take the next steps with us.

Do not let your dreams die.

CHAPTER 1
THE MIND DUMP

"From a small seed a mighty trunk may grow."
– Aeschylus

Welcome to *"The Mind Dump."* This is the beginning portion of your direct hands-on experience and your first step toward further identifying and achieving the wants, dreams, and fantasies you desire.

This is the first exercise of your goal-setting processes and it is primarily designed to help you identify exactly what it is that you might want to achieve. It is critical to be mindful that when it pertains to writing down our goals, we often inadvertently limit ourselves. We may overthink or feel as though the goals we are setting may be too big, or even too small for us.

In this portion of your book, you will be solidifying all of the possible things you may want to obtain, experience, feel, or accomplish. There should be no overthinking, no cutting yourself short, and definitely no leaving anything off the table.

A study performed by a psychology professor at the Dominican University in California, Dr. Gail Matthews, reflected that we are forty-two percent more likely to achieve our goals if we write them down on a regular basis as it helps boost our motivation, improves our focus, reduces our stress levels, and gives us a way to track our progress.

A separate study done by New York University's and University of Hamburg's Gabriele Oettingen, Free University Berlin's Karoline Schnetter, and University of Konstanz's Hyeon-ju Pak, found that people who wrote down their goals, identified potential obstacles, and uncovered solutions to those obstacles were more successful in achieving their goals than those who did not engage in this type of planning.

This supports that when we can see our goals visually, and when we can more effectively plan our approaches, it directly affects how we take action. Once we see our goals written down, we can begin to organize them (which we will help you do in the upcoming chapters), thereby allowing us to improve our focus and analyze which goals are of higher importance and priority than others. One of Justin's former colleagues, Barbara Schneidermayer, wisely teaches, "You must follow the three P's: Prior Proper Planning." It is imperative that we learn how to develop our organizational skills and that we understand the benefits associated with being adequately prepared in our approaches.

In summary, as it relates to your goals, you are more likely to be motivated and productive if you can visually see exactly what it is you have to do instead of just leaving the thoughts floating around aimlessly in your mind. This key point however does not negate the prodigious power of visualization techniques which we will be reviewing in the upcoming chapters. Before you start *"The Mind Dump,"* we strongly suggest you find a space by yourself, free of distractions. Feel free to play calming or uplifting music during this exercise. Instrumental or classical music is recommended as it has scientifically been shown to reduce stress and anxiety, enhance your performance, help you focus, and boost your memory. Once you are ready, let's go ahead and start *"The Mind Dump."*

We want you to begin this exercise by thinking of every single thing you feel you currently need or want, and need or want to do. This means everything you need to do from a task standpoint, all of the goals you want to accomplish, and even material items you desire to obtain. These thoughts can range from the items you feel may need to be on your personal to-do list, all the way to experiences or materials which may be on your bucket list.

Again, do not limit yourself, overthink, or sell yourself short here. These dreams and wants can be as small as washing or cleaning out your car, or as significant as wanting a new car, to becoming the leader of your country. Research supports that human beings are more tribal and communal in nature, and many of us will repress our best selves in order to fit into our communities and into the collective status quo. We urge you not to fall into the trap of limiting yourself to fit in or to set goals that others suggest for you solely for the purpose of fulfilling their own agendas for you. For *"The Mind Dump,"* there is no such thing as thinking too big.

Is there a vacation you have always wanted to go on? How about a dream car you have always wanted? Maybe there is something you have always wanted to do for someone significant in your life? What about connecting with someone you have been talking yourself out of contacting? We want you to know and understand that all of your needs and wants do not have to be materialistic.

Here are just a few examples of items that can be included in your "Mind Dump":
- Wash My Car
- Get a New Car
- Do My Laundry
- Hire a Maid
- Learn a New Language
- Travel to Europe
- Find a Romantic Partner
- Lose Weight
- Create & Implement a Workout Plan
- Write a Book
- Make More Money
- Start a Gratitude Journal
- Volunteer More
- Start My Own Business

A few other keys to success for this exercise: do not worry about your thoughts being organized in any particular order. We will start organizing them in the later chapters after your *"Mind Dump"* is complete. Do your best to be as specific as possible with your thoughts and goals. If you only have general ideas for what it is you want to do, that is alright, too. Write them all down. Take as much time as you need to complete *"The Mind Dump"* and do not stop until you can no longer think of anything further to add to your list. You may end this exercise and later think of something else you want to add, especially as you continue reading into all of the details of *"The 10 Categories of Life."* If or when that happens, that's good, just go back and add it. This particular list is not ever intended to be set in stone. You can always add to it or adjust it at any time, and you likely always will be, as our lives, desires, and circumstances are ever changing.

Performing this exercise more than once and putting any new items on one master list can also be helpful, as different moods and settings may help spark new ideas. You will know you are finished when you cannot think of anything else to add and when you may simultaneously feel an overall sense of relief that everything is all out of your head. If you happen to catch yourself feeling overwhelmed with everything that is written on your list, that is okay, too. We will be providing you with solutions that will help you resolve that feeling as you continue along.

So, before continuing any further in this book, please find that quiet space, grab a pen (or a pencil so that you can more easily make adjustments) and get to work. We highly recommend you do this exercise on paper as opposed to electronically as it helps prompt you to use the more creative, right hemisphere of your brain.

Also, research suggests using red-colored pens or pencils can help with paying more attention to detail and with memorizing information while the use of blue colors can help stimulate more creative thinking.

This is an exciting journey you are now embarking upon, the process of "planting your seeds" (your thoughts and ideas) into reality.

(Authors' Note: If you do not wish to write in your copy of this book, or if you need a fresh template, please feel free to download this template separately by visiting www.TiltingTheBalance.com/Templates).

THE MIND DUMP

CHAPTER 2
THE SELF, CORE VALUES, & BELIEF SYSTEMS

"When you change the way you look at things, the things you look at change."
– Dr. Wayne Dyer

In the first category of *"The 10 Categories of Life,"* you will be exploring yourself, your core values, and personal belief systems. To clarify, this means how we each view ourselves as individuals, how we view our own personal beliefs about ourselves and our moral characters, what core values in life we believe in, cherish, and appreciate, and what personal beliefs we have regarding how we should operate and live our lives.

This category is all about your internal views of your very own internal world and of the external world around you. What we find to be most interesting though is how your internal views may very well control your external reality...

The following poem titled, "Thinking" by Walter D. Wintle, accurately depicts what we are working to explain here in this chapter:

If you think you are beaten, you are
If you think you dare not, you don't
If you like to win, but think you can't
It's almost certain you won't.
If you think you'll lose, you're lost
For out of the world we find,
Success begins with a fellow's will
It's all in the state of mind
If you think you are outclassed, you are
You've got to think high to rise,
You've got to be sure of yourself before
You can ever win a prize.
Life's battles don't always go
To the stronger or faster man,
But soon or late the man who wins
Is the man who thinks he can.

In the *"Introduction"* of this book, we both introduced and recommended learning more about the concept of the *"Law of Attraction."* The *"Law of Attraction"* is a philosophy that people's internal thoughts, feelings, and emotions aid in dictating their external reality. The key principle is, if we can control our thoughts, feelings, emotions, and actions to remain positive in nature, we can create a more positive reality for ourselves, whereas negative thinking, feelings, emotions, and actions will likely bring us more negative and undesired outcomes as a direct consequence. The element of experiencing positive feelings and emotions is probably the most important aspect to the "*Law of Attraction*," and to living the most positive lives we possibly can in general.

It is difficult for us to think positively when we are feeling negatively, and it can be just as challenging to feel positively when we are thinking negatively. In a major way, what we feel is what, and who, we are. Part of our mission as you go along is to give you the understanding and resources you need to identify and break free from any of the negative thought and feeling cycles you may be experiencing.

In the Dr. Joe Dispenza book we'd previously mentioned, *Breaking the Habit of Being Yourself: How to Lose Your Mind and Create a New One*, he writes, "You can't think one way and feel another and expect anything in your life to change. The combination of your thoughts and feelings is your state of being. Change your state of being and change your reality." He reviews that our personality traits are composed of how we think, act, and feel, and are most often based on our past emotions (where he defines emotions as being the end products of any experiences). He continues that our personalities are anchored in the past, and how over a period of weeks, our emotions turn into moods, over months, they turn into temperaments, and how those feelings sustained for a period of several years form strong personality traits. Our bodies go into a cycle of thinking and feeling, then feeling and thinking, cycling the emotions that have become our personalities.

Many of us are spending too much time experiencing negative thoughts, feelings, and emotions due to our direct past memories, experiences, our perspectives on how we may view specific circumstances in our lives, or how we are anticipating events that may or may not ever happen in the future. Michael Singer, author of *Living Untethered: Beyond the Human Predicament,* says, "The moment in front of you is not bothering you, you're bothering yourself about the moment in front of you." What he is saying is that we put ourselves in negative emotional states when we do not need to be in them, all because of how we have been programmed throughout our lives by our past experiences.

In order for us to change our lives, we must first learn how to change our personalities.

To change our personalities, physical realities, and subsequently, our lives, we must learn how to change our emotional states, move from our past, and change the emotions that we have memorized. In essence, we cannot expect to experience different results when we are thinking, feeling, and doing the exact same things that are affecting the results we are currently experiencing now. This is why it is so critical for us to understand our emotions and how to maneuver through past traumas and present addictions. We need to learn how to create a new mind to think about new ways of being, and we will review in more detail about how to do this as you continue along throughout this book.

As you continue to read, keep in mind also that as human beings, we tend to only believe in the things we experience through our senses. We can find it challenging to believe in certain concepts we have not seen, heard, smelled, tasted, touched, or directly experienced ourselves. Through our direct experiences as the authors, we believe that regardless of whether or not you may be more religiously or scientifically inclined, biased, or indifferent, all of the wisdom and action guides assembled in this book can help you draw and create the successful results you desire.

This is why taking action and gaining direct experience is so pertinent, and why it is not only about making shifts in our personalities but also in our identities. Our personalities are the combination of characteristics and qualities that we possess with which we use to define ourselves as individuals. Our identities, however, are defined more as direct self perspectives of the qualities, traits, and characteristics we have and how they impact who we believe we are as individuals. Where it can include and even overlap with our personalities, our identities generally include the self beliefs and perspectives of who we are relative to our genders, sexes, sexual orientations, races, ethnicities, social classes, abilities and disabilities, professions, and other variables such as our relationship, religious, familial, and citizenship statuses. Our collective actions and behaviors can define our identity, and our identities can guide our behaviors, dictate how and why we make specific choices, and influence our actions. Certain aspects of our identities can likely change over time, and many dynamics of our identities can be reinforced or modified by the direct actions we take.

As it pertains to consciously changing our realities, when we can learn how to positively change our identities around the views that are causing us to make decisions that may not be the most beneficially serving us, we can further modify our actions, our habits, and change our lives for the best. In a nutshell, there is tremendous power in becoming consciously aware of the actions you are taking solely because you identify with and believe you are the type of person who takes those specific actions. It can make it much easier to take appropriate action when you believe in your core that you are the type of person who specifically performs the types of actions you want to take.

Our society also tends to be hyperfocused on the external, material world around us. We can over concern ourselves about what we may or may not have, may not have accomplished, compare ourselves to others, or worry about what others may or may not directly think about us. To quote Dr. Joe Dispenza again: "Wherever you put your thoughts and awareness becomes your reality." And, "You, as a human being, have the freedom to place your awareness on anything." The bottom line is, your perception of both your internal and the external world around you is your reality, and you have the option to choose what you wish to focus on, and what you choose to do.

Whether or not you choose to buy into the teachings and philosophies of the "Law of Attraction," as the authors of Tilting The Balance™, our personal core values and beliefs are that these concepts are the absolute essence of our reality. One of the greatest minds of our era, Nikola Tesla, is quoted having said, "If you want to find the secrets of the universe, think in terms of energy, frequency and vibration."

Regardless, positive thoughts, feelings, and emotions are substantially better than negative thoughts, feelings, and emotions for a myriad of scientifically supported reasons. It is for these reasons we highly suggest harnessing the power that comes along with positive thinking. In this section, we are going to review how you can identify the areas in your life where you may find your current thinking, core values, or belief systems might not be serving you the most positively. We are also going to provide some proven strategies for how you can begin to transform your thinking, feeling, and quite possibly... your entire reality.

Let us introduce what we term as *"The 10 Fundamentals of Self-Love"*:

1. Self-Awareness
2. Self-Accountability
3. Affirmations
4. Visualizations
5. Meditation
6. Gratitude
7. Physical Health
8. Mental Health
9. Social Influence
10. Routines & Boundaries

We believe these fundamental principles are crucial to understand and appreciate as you begin your goal-setting processes. They are scientifically supported ways to aid you in successfully meeting your goals and achieving your dreams.

THE FIRST FUNDAMENTAL OF SELF-LOVE: SELF-AWARENESS

"Rather than being your thoughts and emotions, be the awareness behind them."
— Eckhart Tolle

If you want to begin seeing things change in your life, you must first begin by seeing things the way they are. This is exactly why self-awareness is our first fundamental of self-love. Unless you understand how things are, it can be rather challenging to understand why they are the way they are and more importantly, how they may need to change.

So, what exactly is self-awareness? Merriam-Webster's Dictionary defines self-awareness as, *"an awareness of one's own personality or individuality."*

Most of what comprises our self-awareness is the concept we have of ourselves, being our own perceptions of us and who we are, our thoughts, feelings, emotions, and generally how we know and understand our personalities, identities, motives, and desires. Where we are self-aware about our environments, bodies, and lifestyles, we need to be cognizant of all the thoughts we think, the feelings we feel, the emotions that govern us, the actions we take, and our intentions behind them. It is imperative for us to become hyper self-aware, not only so that we may better understand ourselves, but also others, and the world around us. The more we understand how we think, feel, emote, and how or why we decide, act, behave, and operate in the ways we do, the more power we have to change our lives and our realities.

There are a vast amount of powerful benefits associated with being self-aware, and here are several ways self-awareness can help you toward changing your reality:

- Developing a strong, positive, growth mindset
- Empowering better, more rational, intelligent, deliberate, and careful decisions
- Recognizing personal strengths and weaknesses
- Increasing focus
- Enhancing communication skills
- Improving understandings of yourself and others
- Focusing on the positives in negative scenarios
- Recognizing personal behavioral patterns and how others' behaviors might affect you
- Accepting external factors that are not in your control
- Understanding how to become a better influence and what influences affect your state of being
- Establishing deeper self-control
- Creating more happiness and better moods
- Developing stronger relationships and social awareness
- & so much more!

Self-awareness can come in many forms. We can become self-aware of our beliefs, our overall sense of consciousness, the consciousness of the world around us, our self-talk, our value systems, or our individual desires and needs. We can become self-aware of the things we do or say, our habits, our thoughts, feelings, behaviors, and emotions about ourselves and others, or even about what others might say, think, or feel about us. We can also become self-aware about our environment, the people or nature around us, or even of things we are aware of about ourselves that no one else is aware of. We can become self-aware about our personality, our identity, about who we really are and our current paradigms, or about who we truly want to become, along with how and why. We can be self-aware of our body, our health, who or what might influence us, and what behaviors, actions, and decisions may aid us in creating any changes or results we desire.

This entire book is designed to help you with calling awareness to all areas of your life so that you can identify the changes or outcomes that you feel you may want or need to create, know how you can create them, and understand why exactly you may believe you want to create them in the first place. We want you to become hyper-aware of the simple fact that the primary reason we want anything in our lives is due to the feelings we believe we will experience when we attain the specific results we want.

It is also important to understand how throughout the entirety of our daily decision-making processes, we are constantly juxtaposing the manners in which we can avoid the feelings of pain versus seeking ways to subsequently experience feelings of pleasure.

Ultimately, our emotions are created as consequences of our body's reactions to thinking and feeling. As we reviewed, when we can change our emotions, we can change our personalities, our identities, and our lives. The way to do this is by changing our thoughts, feelings, emotions, decisions, and actions through becoming self-aware.

From an excerpt in "Mysteries of the Mind: Is your unconscious making your everyday decisions?" by Marianne Szegedy-Maszak (2/28/05, US News): "According to cognitive neuroscientists, we are conscious of only about five percent of our cognitive activity, so most of our decisions, actions, emotions, and behavior depends on the ninety-five percent of brain activity that goes beyond our conscious awareness. From the beating of our hearts to pushing the grocery cart and not smashing into the kitty litter, we rely on something that is called the adaptive unconscious, which is all the ways that our brains understand the world that the mind and the body must negotiate." This means we are only consciously aware for an average total of just over an hour each day.

Additional studies performed by cognitive psychologists, neurobiologists, and others have indicated that as low as forty percent up to that same ninety-five percent level of our human behavior in being what we think, say, and do overall, falls into the category of habit and more unconscious awareness, which we will elaborate more about later when we review the Routines & Boundaries chapter.

There is actually a very good reason for this. Our brains are always working to be more efficient for us. Charles Duhigg gave great examples of why this is in his book, *The Power of Habit* (which we highly recommend as it is a fascinating read). One of the best examples he provided was about the process of first learning how to operate new motor vehicles. For most who have experienced operating a motor vehicle, the first time we get into a new and unfamiliar one, we start by working to become aware of its components. We look for the ignition switches, the seat belts, the radio dials, the windshield wipers, A/C and window controls, seat adjusters, shifters, and the list can go on. The first time we experience being in a new vehicle, it takes a tremendous amount of brain power for us to process these things. Eventually, if we operate this same motor vehicle numerous times, our brains are designed to govern our habits and create more efficiency for us to have more power to focus on other things. Automaticity is the cognitive quality that saves us from having to relearn all of those steps every time we go to operate our motor vehicles, including relearning how to drive every time. It allows us to perform behaviors without having to think through and focus on each individual step, which explains how we are able to live the majority of our daily lives so unconsciously aware. These same principles can be applied to numerous repeat functionalities of our daily or usual operations. The beauty of the basis of our reality is that we do have the ability to consciously raise our levels of awareness, to change our habits, and recreate our paradigms. We will provide proven strategies for how to successfully do this as you continue along.

The reality is, yesterday has come and gone and tomorrow is not real or yet promised. The only thing that exists is what is happening here and now, in the present moment. Becoming self-aware in the **now** is a key factor in changing your life.

(Authors' Note: An amazing book on developing a heightened sense of self-awareness is Emotional Intelligence 2.0 by Dr. Travis Bradberry and Dr. Jean Graves. Several great reads on staying in the present moment are The Power of Now: A Guide to Spiritual Enlightenment and A New Earth: Awakening to Your Life's Purpose both by Eckhart Tolle, and The Untethered Soul: The Journey Beyond Yourself along with Living Untethered: Beyond the Human Predicament, both by Michael Singer. There are many other powerful books on this concept as well. Find these books available for purchase by visiting www.TiltingTheBalance.com/OurFavoriteBooks).

Sharing some wisdom again from Dr. Joe Dispenza, we are what we are, where we are, and who we are all because of what we individually believe about ourselves. Our beliefs are the composition of the thoughts we keep consciously or unconsciously accepting as the law in our lives. We must learn how to become more observant of ourselves, others, and the world around us. We must do this by becoming more metacognitive (that is having more awareness and understanding of our own thought processes), by closely monitoring our thoughts, welcoming stillness, and focusing more attention on our behaviors and how certain elements in our environment may trigger emotional responses. As he stated, "If you want to create a new self, you first have to stop being the old self."

As part of the self-transformation process, understand that neuroscience suggests the emotions we experience in the now are designed to call our attention about what we may perceive as good, bad, or indifferent. They provide us with insight as to what may be happening in our environments and what may or may not be right or working in our lives. Our emotions are intuitive processes taking place for us, and are not things that are actually happening to us. Stifling our thoughts, feelings, and emotions in unhealthy ways is one of the worst things we can do for ourselves and for our optimal personal growth and development. When we utilize potential self-destructive coping mechanisms such as abusing substances, distractions, or other avoidance strategies in order to escape our emotions, it can result in experiencing further unwanted feelings. It can also lead to greater consequences such as addictions, health complications, unhealed traumas, and even death. It is so important to be aware that what we are feeling is not always permanent, and to know that listening to our feelings can serve as a valuable guide to presenting meaningful insight into our world. This supports the power of being present and learning to pay attention to these insights as they occur. Our emotions are not always rational, and it is up to us to be aware of whether or not our emotions are warranted in our initial evaluation of a specific situation. If they are, we must work to identify whether or not they are accurate in their perception or understanding of each specific situation we are involved in. You must understand that you are in control of your emotions; not the other way around.

The unfortunate reality is that too many people around the world do not understand these concepts, and are therefore allowing their emotions to control them. This is what is leading the vast majority of our interpersonal and social issues across humanity as a collective whole. When all of us can learn to become masters of controlling our emotions, as opposed to allowing ourselves to be controlled by them, we can master the art of creating a better world for all of us **together**. Your mastery of these concepts and of how to implement them not only takes you one step closer toward creating the life you desire, but also toward creating a new and improved paradigm. When you can master the art of listening to your thoughts and feelings, and recognizing your emotions to help you identify their rationality, this is a great step in the right direction toward building the skill of emotional intelligence.

Possessing higher emotional intelligence empowers you to determine whether or not you may need to modify specific thoughts, feelings, attitudes, behaviors, actions, decisions, indecisions, reactions, perspectives, influences, habits, or other potential variables that may not be positively serving you. The key is to listen to yourself objectively, and to use the insights to influence what actions you may need to take in order to create the results you are looking for. As you experience specific emotions and become aware of them as they onset, you can lessen their intensity and increase your self-control. You need to recognize your physiology, tonality, behaviors, or any other actions you are eliciting as you experience those emotions. These variables will aid you in increasing your emotional quotient (EQ), meaning your measured levels of emotional intelligence.

You also want to ask yourself how you are thinking, feeling, and how you know you feel the ways you do. For example, how do you know you are feeling happy? Is there a smile on your face or are you laughing? You must learn to identify how your emotions make you feel physically. Is your heart rate increasing or do you notice a change in your breathing patterns? Do you have butterflies in your stomach or warming sensations throughout your body?

Understanding how to tune into your emotional awareness can help you feel more positive, react more accordingly, and can prevent you from overreacting or jumping to immediate conclusions. In this light, you must work toward becoming aware of the thoughts, feelings, and emotions that are not positively serving you in the now so that you can become aware of how to appropriately change them for the best.

(Authors' Note: Another dynamic to understand is how our bodies and minds work together in creating our emotional states, and how when we smile or frown as examples, our bodies and minds react and release certain chemicals. These chemical reactions can even be sparked through our mere imaginations. This is why we must learn to be in control of our thoughts and emotions, not just because they affect how we see ourselves, our worlds, and how others might see us, but also due to how the constant overproduction of specific chemicals (such as cortisol or adrenaline as examples) can have consequential impacts on our overall physical and mental health. The goal is for us to find the best ways to think, feel, and act that will boost the levels of serotonin, dopamine, oxytocin, endorphins, and other more feel-good chemicals within our bodies and minds).

As you begin to focus on developing a heightened sense of self-awareness through being conscious in the present moment and through becoming more aware of your emotions, we want you to be mindful of your self-talk. Since your emotions are a byproduct of your body's reaction to thinking, the awareness of your self-talk and underlying thoughts is a great place to begin recognizing and reframing your current driving emotions and belief systems.

Self-talk is defined as one's thoughts or dialogue directed at oneself. These include thoughts or words which are said internally or expressed outwardly. Self-talk is that inner dialogue we continuously have with ourselves. It is our voice inside of our heads that is either criticizing, judging, or second guessing ourselves, or that is encouraging us, lifting us up, or praising our actions. Where sometimes we cannot always control exactly what this voice says, we can certainly learn to control how we choose to react to it.

A great early step in mastering self-awareness is by learning how to observe your self-talk to become hyper-aware of your thoughts, along with the feelings and emotions that may be associated with them. We want you to experience the power associated with the understanding that your thoughts are not **you.**

(Authors' Note: Again, we recommend reading Emotional Intelligence 2.0 by Dr. Travis Bradberry and Dr. Jean Graves and The Untethered Soul: The Journey Beyond Yourself by Michael Singer, as well as the books, As a Man Thinketh by James Allen and, What to Say When You Talk to Yourself by Dr. Shad Helmstetter, as they all explore in depth the power of self-talk and how to stay mentally healthy. To find these books available for purchase, visit www.TiltingTheBalance.com/OurFavoriteBooks).

When you can begin to view your thoughts this way and learn how to monitor them as an observer, in lieu of identifying with them, this newfound awareness will move you from looking at your thoughts as if they are a part of you to knowing they are merely your reaction to what is happening in the world around you.

Cognitive behavioral therapy (CBT) is a common form of mental health therapy that is structured on the belief that our thoughts create our emotions. Situations are interpreted through our thoughts, thus leading to the eventual creation of our emotions. CBT is rooted on the emphasis that we can change and control our emotions by changing and controlling our thoughts. This supports why monitoring our self-talk is a strong starting point toward creating personal change.

As we have explained, our perpetual emotional responses to our thoughts and how we decide to continuously act as a subsequent result will shape our personalities, identities, and realities. So when you can master the art of monitoring your thoughts as a conscious observer of them, instead of identifying with them as being a direct part of you, this awareness will help empower you to not immediately emotionally react to any of your thoughts. As you begin to become more aware of your thoughts and self-talk, and actively begin listening to the words you are saying to yourself, we want you to process them as if they were being said aloud to someone else, paying close attention to any thoughts you may be internalizing. This practice can help you in identifying any problem thinking areas in your life and can provide answers to pertinent questions about what changes you feel may need to be made.

Several additional strategies for developing further self-awareness are keeping self-awareness journals to better learn your triggers and responses, delving into books or educational materials on the topic, taking psychometric tests, seeking or entering into mentorships, receiving direct mental health therapies, asking trusted sources how they may view you, or actively looking for opinions that differ from your own that may challenge you to critically think.

Another amazing strategy in realizing deeper self-awareness is via the processes of goal-setting. Writing down your key plans or anything significant that you may want to accomplish, indicating priority levels for any necessary tasks, and tracking your progress for any actions taken along the way, will all help you discover any challenges or obstacles that may be in your way when you do not hit the goals you set or get the results you desire. Elevated self-awareness can also uncover whether or not you are overcomplicating aspects of your life, if you are being overly self-critical, or if you are allowing limiting beliefs or irrational fears to hold you back from performing specific actions.

Here are some questions you can ask yourself to help increase your self-awareness:
- What personality traits or qualities do you like or dislike about yourself?
- Are you eliciting approval-seeking, people-pleasing behavior or seeking validation from others?
- Are you performing self-destructive actions and behaviors?
- Are you experiencing addictions, dependency, or codependency issues?
- Are you aware of your traumas, insecurities, triggers, vices, and coping mechanisms?
- How do your thoughts make you feel and what do they influence you to believe about yourself, your identity, and your reality?
- What is your motivation and your why?
- Are you procrastinating, being avoidant, feeling overwhelmed, or apathetic?
- How can you best manage your emotions and what moves you into positive or negative states?
- What stress management strategies may best serve you?
- Are you doing everything you can to do and be your best for yourself and for others?

Listening to your thoughts and seeking to understand your emotions is where it all begins. Since our collective thoughts, feelings, and emotions are what create our self, our core values, and our belief systems, we have compiled a framework within *Tilting The Balance*™ that will help you create a deeper sense of self-awareness in order to better understand yourself and others, uncover your deepest dreams and desires, and recognize how to most effectively take directive action toward achieving what you want.

As we review this material, we want you to write down any negative or limiting thoughts, complaints, or beliefs that you may think, feel, or identify with as you go along. Do not worry, we are not going to continue focusing on these negative thoughts, feelings, and emotions. We are simply going to point out their very existence so that you can begin to do the work necessary to transform them into more positive ones if you so choose.

For example, as you are reading this section, you may most likely identify and relate upfront with being either a more positive or negative person overall. If you feel you are further on the spectrum of being a positive person, then you are already moving on the right path.

In the event you do find yourself having more tendencies of experiencing negative thinking, feelings, and emotions, do not fret, as we are quite unsure if there is any one human being who is always positive in their own mind one hundred percent of the time. The key though is to strive to be in a positive state of thought and emotion as close to one hundred percent of the time as possible. This is the primary reason why we are exploring a variety of ideas and actions that can help positively transform your constant and persistent thoughts, feelings, and emotions.

If you do feel that your life is in the best place it can possibly be in, that everything is one-hundred-percent perfect and that you have it all figured out, then we challenge you to use this book as a refresher to help further validate those beliefs for you. With so many options and opportunities in this world, and with so many vast possibilities for all that we can create and experience, it is hard for us to believe there is any one individual who is so solely complacent that may not be able to contribute more toward creating a better world for themselves or for those around them.

We are aware that the majority of individuals have the ability to continue to improve the quality of their lives and their experiences, to further grow and advance themselves, and to utilize more of their current means to contribute greater resources for others' time, knowledge, experiences, and material needs.

(Justin's Note: Here are some helpful insights that may prompt deeper creative thinking. One of the first questions I was asked when I began my entrepreneurial journey was a particularly daunting one: What are you passionate about? At that stage in my life, I had no clear answer. I spent months reflecting, searching for direction, and eventually realized that my past jobs and experiences all pointed to one consistent theme. I enjoyed helping others. That realization led to a new question: How could I build a life centered around helping others?

Years later, I came to understand that my journey was not just about passion but about purpose. Passions often evolve as we grow, much like relationships. It is rare to fall in love instantly. Uncovering what we want or love most often takes time, effort, and experience.

Your next step is to define both personal and professional mission statements that clarify your life's purpose, along with a vision statement that captures the bigger picture of what you are working toward. To help guide you through this process, I will share my own as examples:

"My personal life's mission is to create opportunities for personal growth, education, and overall achievement through positive role modeling."

"'My professional mission is to provide educational and fiscal resources to empower individuals and businesses to achieve health, wealth, and fulfillment."

"My personal vision is to create a world where individuals recognize their true potential, pursue their dreams with clarity, and live with purpose and fulfillment."

At my core, I want to make the world a better place by setting a positive example, creating opportunities, and providing meaningful solutions. I am especially passionate about business and education as avenues to empower individuals, since it equips them to better uplift and support others.

One of the most valuable tools that helped me refine my purpose was Ikigai, a concept I discovered in a course from Jeff Lerner's ENTRE Institute. Ikigai is an ancient Japanese philosophy that translates to "a reason for being." In Japanese, Iki means "life," and gai refers to value or worth. This framework encourages deep reflection by asking four key questions: What do you love? What are you good at? What can you be paid for? What does the world need?

If you would like further guidance on how to craft your own mission and vision statements, visit www.TiltingTheBalance.com/Statements. There, we have also provided a powerful template for creating a Chief Aim Statement, a clearly defined statement of purpose that can reprogram both your subconscious mind and conscious reality. Highly successful individuals such as Abraham Lincoln, Thomas Edison, Bruce Lee, Warren Buffett, and Elon Musk have all used this practice to shape their destinies. Napoleon Hill explored this concept in detail in Think and Grow Rich, demonstrating its effectiveness in turning ambition into tangible results).

We believe this is sufficient enough information to get you properly moving along in your journey of understanding self-awareness and change. The big questions now are whether or not you really want to change or make any changes, and what your motivations may be behind actually wanting to create change. Once you are aware that you want to make changes, there will likely be actionable steps to become aware of, and associated actions that you may need to take to set in motion the changes you so desire.

Tilting The Balance™ is here to be your guide for mastering your awareness so that you can experience the most meaningful, fulfilled life, complete by your design.

THE SECOND FUNDAMENTAL OF SELF-LOVE: SELF-ACCOUNTABILITY

"...and the truth will set you free."
– John 8:32 NIV

As we become fully self-aware, we must learn how to take personal responsibility for all of the things we become aware of that are within the realms of our personal control. Self-accountability is the single most integral part of self-love and personal success. Without personal accountability, without being personally responsible, any awareness we create around changes that need to be made may be meaningless if we are unwilling to be responsible for them and most especially, responsible for making them.

Accountability is defined in Merriam-Webster's Dictionary as, *"the quality or state of being accountable, especially: an obligation or willingness to accept responsibility or to account for one's actions."* Accountability is about taking responsibility for our lives. It is about knowing that it is up to each of us as individuals to create the changes we strive for, owning and accepting that we are each who, what, and where we are solely based on our individual thoughts, feelings, emotions, attitudes, behaviors, and actions. We are also directly impacted by the decisions we do or do not make, our reactions and perspectives to outer influences, our collective habits, paradigms, or any other potential variables we may have allowed to affect us up to this point. It is important to note that there is a major difference between personal accountability (meaning being accountable to ourselves as individuals), and the varying levels of accountability we may share in our dealings with others.

Self-accountability is so important because without it, we will likely never achieve our true desires (or retain them if we do), complete the tasks we need to, grow as individuals, or heal in the ways we must. As we become aware of our thoughts, feelings, emotions, attitudes, behaviors, actions, decisions, indecisions, reactions, perspectives, influences, habits, and paradigms, we must learn to take responsibility for them. It is important to learn from our past and present mistakes and "failures" to better prevent new ones from occurring, and to use them toward creating the futures we so desire. Self-accountability is all about taking control of our lives, not allowing life to take control of us, and not letting ourselves give in to any excuses. We are each responsible for the majority of the cycles and circumstances we experience in our lives; good, bad, or indifferent.

So, how do you properly implement accountability into your own life? One of the best ways is through finishing this book, completing all of the exercises we present to you, and by actually applying everything you will read. We are providing you with the framework you need to be successful if you can be accountable enough to yourself, accept your responsibility in the way things currently are, and be responsible enough to understand your roles in creating your life the way you want it to be.

With that, what are you accountable for exactly? We can tell you from firsthand experience, it is more than most of us tend to be aware of and, once we are, it is usually more than we are willing to admit or accept to ourselves or especially others. First, we will review what you are not responsible for, since that is a much shorter and easier list to digest and accept.

You are not responsible for other peoples' thoughts, feelings, emotions, attitudes, or behaviors. Nor are you responsible for whatever actions they take, decisions or indecisions they make, reactions, habits, or paradigms they may have, their perspectives or influences that are affecting their lives, or the beliefs they may hold about you.

However, understand that you do have responsibility in your influences toward those dynamics for others. You may also have a heightened sense of responsibility for others in the event you are in specific leadership roles or when other applicable, extenuating circumstances may apply.

You are limited in your responsibility and control over external circumstances. You may not always be able to predict unforeseen circumstances, situations, obstacles, or setbacks. However, you are responsible for how you think, feel, and act once these challenges arise. You are responsible for doing what you can, where you can, how you can, and when you can and for understanding where the lines of personal accountability are to be drawn in general. We could venture deep down the rabbit hole about these types of scenarios but will keep it limited to briefly referencing specific examples such as weather occurrences or other acts from mother nature, freak accidents, the media, what others may opt to do, etc.

The last thing is, you are not entirely responsible for your own individual success. As abstract as this may seem, where the entire emphasis of our book is all about how to create the life of your dreams and how to identify and create the success you desire, you cannot always control the outside variables that may play into the overall attainment of your personalized vision of success. Your vision of success is also subject to change. Success is not always in your control and can sometimes depend on external factors or people in order to play out favorably. Sometimes, life is all about timing versus opportunity, where both variables must synchronize and work together harmoniously. That is not always in our control, as sometimes we can attract the right opportunities or people at not so opportune times or, sometimes the timing may be right but the opportunities are not, nor even may they yet be present at all. As Macho Man Randy Savage so wisely said in a television interview, *"There's one guarantee in life in that there are no guarantees."*

Outside of those variables, everything else pretty much completely and solely rests upon **you.** You are ultimately accountable for yourself, and that is the most real and difficult truth for most of us to accept and appreciate.

With that, we have done our best to put together a comprehensive list (listed in no particular order of importance) of what you are responsible for, though a more complete list could be written into an entirely separate book.

You are responsible for:

- Your own happiness and for creating the life you want
- Your current mindset, circumstances, and present reality
- Becoming metacognitive, hyper self-aware, and honest with both yourself and others
- Developing and strengthening a growth mindset
- Selecting and taking care of your responsibilities
- Your personal growth and development
- Acquiring knowledge and wisdom
- Your relationship with yourself and your relationships with others
- Your power and energy, physical, mental, and emotional health, self-care, and self-worth
- What you put on and into your mind, body, and spirit
- Being proactive versus reactive
- Discovering your desires, dreams, motivations, your purpose, and your why
- Staying motivated, committed, determined, dedicated, disciplined, courageous, consistent, resilient, and persistent
- Knowing when to persevere, change course, reset, or restart in your approaches
- Juxtaposing optimism versus practicality along with instant versus delayed gratification
- Managing your emotions, emotional responses, stressors, and exhibiting self-control
- Critically thinking and expanding your intellectual and emotional intelligence
- Developing self-confidence and personal empowerment
- Identifying problems and uncovering solutions
- Your individual performance and progression
- Developing love, compassion, patience, and empathy toward yourself and others
- Learning how to forgive yourself, others, and how to let go of negative attachments
- Eliminating validation, approval-seeking, self-sacrificing behaviors, along with self-critical, self-limiting beliefs
- Learning how to effectively listen and communicate
- Overcoming uncertainty, fears, traumas, guilts, insecurities, and addictions
- Reeducating yourself to surmount learned helplessness, cognitive dissonance, passive-aggressiveness, and any counterproductive prior beliefs or conditioning
- Operating with humility and integrity, being authentic and genuine in everything you do and say
- Your priorities, focus, preparation, and organization
- Understanding your conscious and subconscious mind, how they work, and how you can best operate them

We could continue on naming everything that you are responsible for in your life. It ultimately comes down to you taking charge. You are in control of your choices and how you choose to respond to your thoughts, feelings, emotions, and the external stimuli and situations dealt to you from others and from life. You must understand the things in your life that cannot be changed, your responsibility in what can be changed, and for deciphering the differences between the two.

The best you can do is your best, to be the best you can be, and to do the best with what you have, doing your best all the while to get what you want and need with the gifted time you are granted while here on this earth. It is up to you to determine and create the impact you want to have in this world and to leave the legacy you want behind. It is up to you to create the appropriate balance in your world by making the right decisions and becoming clear about your desires to create change, by changing how you think, how you feel, what you believe, how you are living, what you are doing, and how you are being.

Whatever has attracted you to this book, we appreciate that you are here. A key element of our mission is to provide you with insight of all the areas in life you have responsibilities in, and to help you understand what areas you can focus on, prioritize, and set goals in to empower you to more effectively create balance and fulfillment for yourself. As we stated, you are responsible for gaining the understandings and taking the necessary actions for how to best apply all of the wisdom we share from "*The 10 Fundamentals of Self-Love*," "*The 10 Categories of Life*," and all of the other insights and exercises we present throughout this book.

You are responsible for making and taking the time to actually complete the steps in this book and for furthering your knowledge from there. The more knowledge you have, the better prepared you will be for new experiences. You are responsible for understanding and applying that principle into your life, for learning and growing as much as you can, and for creating the change and life that you want. You are responsible for **you**.

The real question is, are you ready to admit, accept, and appreciate the truth, take full accountability for yourself, and become totally responsible for your life?

THE THIRD FUNDAMENTAL OF SELF-LOVE: AFFIRMATIONS

"Believe you can and you're halfway there."
– Theodore Roosevelt

Affirmations are positive statements that can assist you in overcoming some of the challenges of negative, non-self-serving, and self-sabotaging thinking.

The key to success with affirmations is to repeat these statements aloud, at least twice daily. Not only must you recite them aloud, but you must also experience how it would feel in the event the statements you are saying aloud were already indeed the truth in your present reality. This is how the power of affirmations can transform your life. As you begin to believe the statements, you will begin to experience the results associated with believing in them, prompting a shift in your physical reality and paradigm.

Therefore, we believe this is one of the best places for you to start. As you continue reading into the next chapters, we encourage you to be self-aware of any negative thoughts, feelings, or beliefs you may have and to write them down. Maybe you will think to yourself that you are not an organized person or that you are not good at time management, as examples. Maybe you will feel that you are not worthy or deserving, or that you will never find the love you desire in the relationships with your family, friends, or romantic interests. You may think you will never make the money you want or that you will never achieve certain goals you wish to accomplish in the business or financial areas of your life. Remember to be ultra self-aware of these thoughts as they come to you in the present moments as you read this book and throughout your days, and make it a practice to write down the thoughts and beliefs that you may identify as not beneficial to the reality you desire. As you continue to become hyper self-aware of your limiting thoughts, feelings, and beliefs, you can begin to change them into more positive perspectives.

There is great power in writing down your negative thoughts, feelings, and beliefs and then seeing and experiencing them visually due to the awareness it will create. The next step is to write down the opposite of your negative statements, written in a more positive light, and especially as an *"I am"* statement. When you use *"I am"* statements, you are using an essential mechanism for further developing your self-love and self-awareness. When you focus these positive statements directly toward yourself by beginning with *"I am,"* you are creating more self-control, inner peace, and an elevated sense of internal being.

When you use these statements, you are taking control of your thoughts, feelings, and beliefs by impressing new, more beneficial views that reduce the effect of negative emotions upon your subconscious mind and change your perspective. They can positively influence who you are, who you want to be, and how you want to feel. As we have reviewed, when you can change your perspective and prompt shifts in your thoughts, feelings, and emotions that can change your personality and identity, you can subsequently change your life.

Affirmations are also an evidence-based practice. "Self-affirmation activates brain systems associated with self-related processing and reward and is reinforced by future orientation"; a study published by the peer-reviewed scientific journal, Social Cognitive and Affective Neuroscience, showed that affirmations objectively measured positive behavior change in study participants and impacted their neural pathways to the brain regions that are most prominently associated with self-processing, reward, and positive valuation.

Even if you are skeptical, what does it hurt to try? Here is how to most efficiently begin the process of incorporating affirmations into your life.

As an example, if you have a thought or belief that you are not good at taking notes, write it down as:

"I am not a good note taker."

For this example, we want you to take a moment to write this sentence on paper, even if you believe you are a good note taker. How did it feel writing that down? Do you see how it feels when you just read that in a possessive, objective form? Say it aloud once and see how it feels. If you believe you are a great note taker, when writing and then reading that example aloud, how did it make you feel? Did it reinforce your positive belief or did it make you question yourself and your abilities? The point here is to draw further awareness to your existing belief systems, and then to discover the most effective ways to positively impress the most optimal self-serving belief systems upon your subconscious mind.

Therefore, what is the exact opposite of not being a good note taker? This is the foundation for how you will structure your affirmations.

You would want your positive affirmation to look something like this:

"I am always a phenomenal note taker."

Write that down as well. How does it feel writing and reading that affirmation? Try stating it aloud and feeling like it is already the truth. If you do not believe it, we assure you, if you keep saying it as a matter of practice, in no time, you most likely will. In our personal experiences, affirmations can work in just the matter of mere days. The trick is to repeatedly recite the affirmations, as only saying them once is not going to make much of a difference in rewiring your subconscious mind. Say you do identify with being a great note taker but not always being one or a phenomenal one, then that positive affirmation example can benefit you as well, right? Would it not be better to always be a phenomenal note taker as opposed to just being a great one? Lastly, if you already believe you are always a phenomenal note taker, then the question is why? Why is that belief so concretely instilled in you?

This is the science in how affirmations work. We tend to not only tell ourselves our beliefs about ourselves, but we also tend to live and to experience them. Too many times, we do not even know where we adopted our beliefs from or why we have them in the first place. If, as an example, always being a phenomenal note taker is not important to you, that is okay. Understand the imperative aspect of affirmations is to focus on the areas where you desire and require the most improvement. It is all about what is most beneficial for you.

What we have found to be the primary formula to successful affirmations is to always make it possessive (I am), to always make it a constant (always), and to use strong, positive adjectives (words such as amazing, astounding, phenomenal, etc.), and then add your desired outcome, being as specific as you can be.

Each affirmation should be like the positive affirmation example we used about note taking with each of your desired outcomes at the end:

"I am always a/an (adjective here) (desired outcome here)."

Here are a few examples of effective affirmations:

"I am always perfectly on time for everything."

"I am always super detailed and organized in all aspects of my life."

"I am always profoundly loved and appreciated by everyone in my world."

We want to emphasize one last major point here. Your negative or self-limiting thoughts may not just be something so simple as, "I am always late," or, "I am unorganized." What you are thinking could be something more deep-seeded such as general feelings of being unwanted, like you do not matter, or that you have little-to-nothing of value to offer. Where this is most likely furthest away from the truth, we all tend to be our own worst critics.

As human beings, we are often more critical of ourselves because we most introspectively see and know what we think. We know what our desires truly are and how we feel about different variables in our lives, yet not all of those factors are put into the world for others to judge. When they are, we may not always get the most qualified judges and/or judgments. The point is, you are often the best judge of your thoughts and your actions. You are the one who is capable of making the changes you want and of attaining the outcomes you desire.

(Authors' Note: A couple of great reads on the power of affirmations are the classics, The Game of Life and How to Play It and Your Word Is Your Wand by Florence Scovel Shinn. You can find all of our recommended books at www.TiltingTheBalance.com/ OurFavoriteBooks. We also encourage you to check out Justin's exciting music project, Affirmation Station Music, where you can find a wide variety of music genres featuring affirmation-based messages designed to help you reprogram your mind, elevate your mood, and reinforce a positive mindset. Visit AffirmationStationMusic.com to explore the collection).

THE FOURTH FUNDAMENTAL OF SELF-LOVE: VISUALIZATIONS

Whatever you hold in your mind on a consistent basis is exactly what you will experience in your life."
– Tony Robbins

Not only is visualizing your dreams through writing down your goals a powerful method, but so is the art of practicing visualization techniques. Visualization is a technique where you create a mental image of a future event in your mind which likely has not yet actually happened. The goal is to imagine yourself in a reality which you desire yourself to be. Not only do you need to imagine yourself in that reality, you also must feel what it would feel like to be in that reality, as we suggested you do earlier in this chapter to harness the power of affirmations. The more clear and detailed you are in your visual realities and the more you are able to feel them to be real, the more viable chances you have of manifesting your visualizations into your actual physical reality.

If this sounds a bit wacky, ask MMA superstar and successful entrepreneur Conor McGregor. Regardless of some of his shenanigans throughout the duration of his Ultimate Fighting Championship (UFC) career, you cannot take away from his overall success and accomplishments. He will tell you all about how he visualized himself successful and driving a Bentley around the streets in California, when in reality he was driving a beater car while broke and living in Ireland. He will also tell you about how when he was a kid, he would visualize himself being in stadiums and arenas filled with people. He talks about how he felt and imagined himself already being the champion of the UFC, and how he visualized himself winning multiple championship belts. Conor will additionally tell you how the things he perpetually focused on and visualized manifested themselves into real, actual results and experiences in his own physical reality. What is even more wild is that he is far from being alone.

Mary Lou Retton, the first to have won the all-around gold medal in gymnastics during the 1984 Olympics, has continuously emphasized how visualization techniques helped her become a gold medalist and world-renowned Olympic Champion. How about Roger Bannister who visualized and felt himself running the first four minute mile? Oprah Winfrey, Arnold Schwarzenegger, Jim Carrey (who wrote a check to himself ten years in advance in the amount of ten million dollars for "acting services rendered" and then received a ten-million-dollar check ten years after for his performance in *Dumb and Dumber*), Tiger Woods, Lebron James, Kobe Bryant, Will Smith, Lady Gaga, Jay Z, and so many others who have used the power of visualization would need to be in a book of their own to even begin skimming the surface of those with similar stories to share.

Our brains have a fascinating system called the "Reticular Activating System" which is a network of neurons responsible for helping to arouse the brain as a whole and to control our wakefulness, our fight-or-flight responses, our capacities to focus, and, most interestingly, how we perceive our worlds around us. This system also filters approximately ninety-nine percent of our sensory input to our brains, particularly for the purpose of protecting our brains from experiencing sensory overload. What is fascinating about how this "filtration" system works is that it prioritizes information we have signaled as important or relevant, whether through repeated attention, emotional significance, or survival value.

When we consistently focus on specific goals through affirmations and visualizations, we are training our brains to flag related opportunities and information as important, making us more likely to notice them. The main premise of the power of visualization is that we can influence what our brains prioritize, helping us to spot new opportunities that will subsequently change our lives and yield us the results we desire.

(Authors' Note: Some powerful reads that delve deeper into these concepts are Living Untethered: Beyond the Human Predicament by Michael Singer, The Divine Matrix by Gregg Braden, The Master Key System by Charles F. Haanel, Think and Grow Rich by Napoleon Hill, Breaking The Habit of Being Yourself by Dr. Joe Dispenza and three short reads by Neville Goddard, Feeling Is the Secret, Out of this World, and The Power of Awareness. As always, you can find these books available for purchase by visiting our website at www.TiltingTheBalance.com/OurFavoriteBooks).

Another fantastic book we recommend reading about the power of visualization techniques is titled, *The New Psycho-Cybernetics* by Dr. Maxwell Maltz. He goes into great depth about the research that has been done using brain imagery and how they can see the process of how visualization works due to neurons in our brains. He explains how these neurons elicit electrically excitable cells that transmit information and are interpreted by the imagination as if they were equivalent to an action occurring in real life.

What this means is that when we go through the process of visualizing an act, our brains generate an impulse that tells the neurons in our brain to actually execute the movement. Through a cluster of cells in our brain called "neural pathways" which work together to create our learned behaviors and memories, they prompt our bodies to behave in such a manner that is congruent to what we imagined.

What is amazing is that we are able to achieve physical results due to our imaginations, and that this phenomena can transpire without us actually having to enact real physical activities. Our brains and bodies do not understand the difference between events we are imagining versus the events we are experiencing in real life.

There are popular experiments out there that support this science as well. Some have been done where athletes were hooked up to electrodes while performing physical tasks and were then instructed to imagine themselves performing those same physical tasks. Interestingly, their bodies reacted similarly to both sets of stimuli. Essentially, their bodies could not decipher what was transpiring in real life versus what was happening in their mere imaginations.

We must master how to use our imaginations to visualize the results and experiences we desire in life and learn how to perpetually feel the feelings of having experienced the results of our deepest desires ahead of actually having experienced them in our physical realities. This is also where we can use the power of gratitude in our visualization practices, feeling thankful and appreciative of the things we want as if we have already received them. This entire concept is the belief system that is centered entirely around the extremely powerful technique of manifestation.

(Justin's Note: One of the biggest dreams I have ever visualized is seeing Tilting The Balance™ become a New York Times® Best Seller. Before the book actually launched, I created a mock cover with the New York Times Bestseller badge and made it the background on my phone screen. Every time I looked at it, I was reminded of what I was building. On the whiteboard in my home, I wrote the affirmation: "I am so happy and grateful now that I am a New York Times Best-Selling author." I read that out loud numerous times until I believed it. I have seen it. I have felt it. I have experienced and committed to it before there was any actual proof.

Visualization gives us a target. Belief and aligned action are what will make it possible. Whatever your goal is, whether it feels big or small, train your mind to see it clearly and feel the emotions of success before it happens. Let those feelings guide your actions. When you live from that place, you can begin to create the outcome ahead of the experience.

The day this book earns that honor, it will not be a coincidence. It will be the result of living this message. It will also be proof that you can do it, too, and that is the real mission).

THE FIFTH FUNDAMENTAL OF SELF-LOVE: MEDITATION

"We cannot solve our problems with the same thinking we used when we created them."
– Albert Einstein

Meditation is a consciousness-changing technique, designed with the intent of encouraging a heightened state of focused attention and awareness.

There are all sorts of forms of meditation, ranging from and not limited to: *Mindfulness Meditation, Spiritual Meditation, Focused Meditation, Movement Meditation, Mantra Meditation, Transcendental Meditation, Progressive Relaxation, Loving-Kindness Meditation, Visualization Meditation, Zen Meditation, Yoga Meditation, Vipassana Meditation, Chakra Meditation, Qigong Meditation, Sound Bath Meditation, and so much more.*

While we will not review in detail the extensive types of meditation in this work, what we want you to understand is the primary goal of meditation, which is to calm and relax the mind so that you can achieve a higher state of self-awareness and consciousness. Some of the potential scientifically proven benefits of meditation include:

· Heightened self-awareness
· Increased emotional and physical health
· Reduced stress levels along with more control over sleep and anxiety
· Assistance with overcoming pain and addictions
· Boosts in memory and attention span
· & much more!

There is great power associated with calming your mind and body through the practice of meditation.

As we have mentioned, our conscious minds, the left hemispheres of our brains, are objective. Our conscious minds are responsible for our short-term memories, our critical and logical thinking, our levels of will power, and pretty much contain all of the thoughts, memories, feelings, and desires that we are aware of in any present moment. It is also the center for speech and language.

However, the right hemispheres of our brains, our subconscious, unconscious minds, are subjective, and do not think or reason independently outside of the commands (or impressions) it receives and obeys from our conscious minds. This mind is also where our long-term memory is held, where we store our self-image, our internal and external belief systems, our imaginations, intuitions, our emotions, values, fears, protective reactions, along with our individual habits, and our collective paradigms. The subconscious mind also controls all of our bodily systems, which is why we do not have to think moment-by-moment about our breathing, heartbeats, fluctuating our body temperatures, regulating our blood flow, generating new cells, etc.

The subconscious mind is designed to store and retrieve data and is not intended to judge or discern any data or input. With an essentially unlimited storage capacity to permanently store everything that has ever happened to us, it works to ensure that you respond appropriately to the programming that it has stored concerning what you have adopted to be the truth about your thoughts, feelings, emotions, and beliefs about your internal and external reality.

It is also interesting to note that the conscious mind responsible for our communication is separate from the subconscious mind that is responsible for our feelings. This disconnect is why it can sometimes be so challenging for us to understand our feelings. It can also stifle our abilities to most effectively communicate them with others.

To best summarize, the observing, conscious mind impresses the subconscious mind while the subconscious mind works to outwardly express the impressions. As we reviewed earlier, it is estimated that our subconscious minds operate up to ninety-five percent of our conscious days. We must learn how to reprogram our subconscious minds. Where affirmations, visualizations, gratitude practices, hypnosis, biofeedback, and even exercise are all effective ways to do this, meditation is an ultra effective measure.

As we have touched on vibrations and frequencies, our brains create brain waves when neurons in our brains communicate with each other. These synchronized electrical pulses operate on different frequencies of electromagnetic energy and our brain waves constantly fluctuate based upon our moods, our activities, and on what we are thinking, feeling, and doing. There are five majorly recognized brain waves, and they are actually all measurable in frequency units of Hertz. There are gamma waves, beta waves, alpha waves, theta waves, and delta waves. These different brain waves aid us in sleeping, in our learning, productivity, decisions, reactions, etc., and are all working together to essentially make our thoughts, emotions, and actions all possible.

Meditation creates changes in our brains' electrical activities, and the practice of meditation itself will stimulate and can even change these waves in our brains. Research also suggests the practice of habitual meditation can stimulate and create those changes even long after the meditations are complete, plus it can positively affect our brain wave activity afterwards for years to come. The goals with meditation are to heighten the state of your brain waves, to relax the mind and body, and to move beyond the conscious, analytical mind to aid you in mastering the idea of being present and understanding that your thoughts are not you.

Incorporating meditation as a routine practice can provide you with many of the benefits we already reviewed and can bring a lot of peace, calmness, relaxation, and balance into your reality. Moreover, when you observe your thoughts to identify and understand the issues in your thinking, you can utilize this awareness to help you reframe your perceptions and perspectives to change your thoughts, your feelings, your personality, identity, actions, paradigms, and your entire reality.

Here is a meditation technique you can use to begin immediately experiencing the benefits of meditation. We recommend you perform this twice or more per day, especially once right upon waking and once just prior to retiring.

MEDITATION TECHNIQUE: COUNTING BACKWARDS

The first step of this exercise is to ensure that you are in a safe, comfortable environment, free of any noise and of all distractions.

The next step is to get into a comfortable position, either sitting or laying down. You will want to close your eyes and begin breathing in through your nose, and out through your mouth, while focusing on the sound of your breath.

With each breath cycle, you are going to begin counting backwards from 10. Breathe in deep through your nose, and breathe out through your mouth, 10... Breathe in deep through your nose, and breathe out through your mouth, 9... Breathe in deep through your nose, and breathe out through your mouth, 8... Repeat this all of the way until you count down to zero.

The significance of counting backwards is so that there is an expiration. This way your mind can begin to quiet. Once you complete the countdown, sit or lay there in the calmness and silence.

Allow yourself to stay in that state as long as you are able to and monitor what kind of thoughts and feelings you may experience.

Again, the goal is to quiet the mind and allow yourself to be free of thought.

(Authors' Note: We also recommend listening to meditations or other positive recordings, such as audiobooks, seminars, or mindful guided content, as you fall asleep. During this time, the brain naturally enters a theta state, which neuroscience has shown to be one of the most receptive periods for absorbing new beliefs and suggestions. It is often compared to a light form of self-hypnosis, commonly used in guided meditation and mental reprogramming practices. Listening to positive input during the theta brainwave cycle can help reprogram your mind while you sleep. Much of this content can be found for free on platforms like YouTube, including guided meditations, affirmations, visualizations, audiobooks, motivational seminars, and more).

THE SIXTH FUNDAMENTAL OF SELF-LOVE: GRATITUDE

"Whatever we think about and thank about we bring about."
– John F. Demartini

One of the most powerful ways of keeping yourself in a positive frame of mind is by harnessing the empowering power of gratitude. When you are in a state of gratitude, it also helps to promote a more healthy and positive mindset. It is much harder to be upset about the things in life that you may not yet have when you are grateful for what you do have.

As author Roy T. Bennett states in his book, *The Light In The Heart*, "Be grateful for what you already have while you pursue your goals. If you aren't grateful for what you already have, what makes you think you would be happy with more." It also tends to be a principle that when you are grateful for what you have, the laws of the universe will bless you with even more for which to be grateful.

There are many ways to utilize the power of gratitude in your life. One way is to create a "Master Gratitude List" where you add as many items to it as possible and then review and add to it on a daily basis.

Other methods include creating a daily gratitude journal where you write a certain number of individual things down that you are grateful for (say twenty as an example) or where you write a shorter list (let's use five as an example) and go into greater detail as to why you are specifically grateful for those things.

As we have reviewed, a primary factor in how we create the realities for ourselves is based directly upon our thoughts and feelings. When we work toward our desires in a state of gratitude and positivity, it reinforces our desires for further positive thoughts and feelings, and it makes it difficult for us to focus on lack, unworthiness, or other limiting emotions that could hold us back mentally, physically, or spiritually.

Oftentimes, we are driven by more conditional emotions, thinking and feeling that things will change or improve when or if something specific occurs. Our thoughts create our feelings, our feelings create our emotions, our emotions create our personalities, our personalities along with our identities create our actions, our paradigms, and this continuum creates our realities. When we can change our perceptions and perspectives, we can change this entire cycle. This is why it is so important to learn how to shift your thoughts to that of being grateful and feeling thankful for what you already do have. The routine practice of gratitude can help you overcome your conditional emotions and aid you in experiencing more non-conditional ones, keeping you in the present moment and feeling less concerned or worried about the past or the future.

We must master the art of accepting what we have and of learning to appreciate exactly where we are. Sometimes, even the most taxing experiences can prepare us for new challenges. Our determination to persevere through our difficulties can even empower us to help others better navigate through their challenges to overcome their struggles in life as well. This is why we must learn how to always be thinking and feeling thankful for the things we currently have, as opposed to thinking or feeling that we can only be happy if or when we have something or when some specific outcome or circumstance occurs. Comprehending and implementing the concept of gratitude will help prevent you from experiencing anxiety, frustration, and other unwanted feelings, and will prompt changes in your thinking, which will lead to changes in your feelings, in your actions, and again, ultimately, in your reality.

This is also why it is so important that we do not compare ourselves to others in the sense of looking at what we do not have, what we have not yet accomplished, or what we have not yet become. Comparison can be the thief of joy and unless we are in a contest of sorts, the only competition we are in is the one with ourselves, competing to be a better version of ourselves in the next moment than we were in the ones prior. Instead, we must appreciate the gifts we already do have in comparison to others and broaden our understanding for how we can use our current resources to give and provide a greater source of gratitude for others in the world. If we are going to compare ourselves to others, then we must do so in a way that makes us feel excited and inspired for both them and ourselves. We must look at others from the perspective that if they can have, do, attain, or embody something that we want, then we either have the potential to have, do, attain, or embody the same or we have the ability to be inspired by others or their capabilities. The magic happens when we can learn to experience gratitude and appreciation for *all* things in life. Even more magic happens when we can learn to feel gratitude and appreciation for the things we want before they actually manifest into our physical realities.

So, can you physically see, hear, speak, stand, or walk? Can you feel physical sensations or do you have control over your motor functions? Do you have strong physical or mental health? Any forms of material wealth? A vehicle? A roof over your head? Electricity or running water? Family, friends, or a significant other? We could go on and on. The point is to reflect on the blessings that you currently have and to understand that even though you may not have all of the same luxuries or experiences that others might, not everyone will likely have the same luxuries or experiences that you might, either. You can find the smallest things to be grateful for, and sometimes, the things that you perceive to be small, are the things that are the biggest to others. It is all about perspective and learning to appreciate the gifts that life has to offer.

(Authors' Note: There are many ways to incorporate gratitude into your daily life. One simple method is to carry a small trinket in your pocket or purse. Each time you happen to touch it, let it serve as a reminder to think of something you feel grateful for. As we mentioned, create a "Master Gratitude List" and make it a practice to view it every morning, evening, or any time you may need a pleasant and powerful reminder. We have even participated in personal group text chats where, each day, we all shared heartfelt lists of at least five things we were grateful for. These are all easy ways to keep your blessings top of mind and your heart centered in a place of love and appreciation).

THE SEVENTH FUNDAMENTAL OF SELF-LOVE: PHYSICAL HEALTH

"It is health which is real wealth and not pieces of gold and silver."
– Mahatma Gandhi

Physical Fitness is also a part of one of *"The 10 Categories of Life."* The fact is, taking care of our physical bodies is one of the single most beneficial things we can do for ourselves as individuals. Every essence of our beings is encompassed within the physical vessels of our bodies.

One of the most proven methods for taking care of our bodies is through the power of physical exercise. Regular exercise is scientifically proven to:

- Increase our lifespan
- Improve our overall levels of both physical and mental health
- Aid in the recovery of addictions
- Improve our memory and general mood
- Increase our energy levels, sleep quality, and sexual performance
- Decrease our levels of anxiety, stress, and pain
- Reduce our risk of ailments and chronic diseases
- Improve our weight, skin, and physical appearance
- Positively benefit all of our body's six major Cardiovascular/Circulatory, Digestive, Nervous, Muscular, Respiratory, and Skeletal Systems

It is absolutely critical that we make the time for ourselves to properly exercise and take care of our physical bodies. While there are some astonishing and hyperintelligent advances in medical technologies, for now anyways, your current physical body is the only body you get.

There are a myriad of effective types of exercises you can do. There is aerobic exercise, balance training, endurance, flexibility, and strength training exercises. You can walk, jog, run, lift weights, perform yoga, swim, dance, bike, hike, row, play sports; the list goes on.

For the benefit of a more potentially prolonged lifespan, we highly recommend you incorporate exercise into your lifestyle.

Not only is regular exercise an aberrant and essential way of taking care of our bodies, but, what we put into our bodies is equally (if not even more) as important. Oxford Language's Dictionary defines "nutrition" as, *"the process of providing or obtaining the food necessary for health and growth."*

Most of us fail to understand and educate ourselves about what the best processes are. We do not take the time to read the labels on the products we buy which we apply topically or put into our mouths and bodies. Remember, our skin, our body's largest organ, is porous and absorbs what we put on it. This is one of the most detrimental mistakes people are making today in regards to their overall levels of health and wellness. Too many foods and products are jam-loaded with ingredients that are scientifically proven to be harmful for us. This is why it is so vital for us to make the time to learn about proper nutrition and understand what our bodies need nutritionally, and why.

It is also important to know that we have a "second brain" located directly in our guts. It is around the size of a small dog's or cat's brain, and it is comprised of about five-hundred-million neurons with forty neurotransmitters similar to those in our brains. Even though this system operates independently from our brains, they do communicate together. This is part of why the foods and products we consume directly affect our brains and bodies, as do the stress levels we experience. Numerous studies support how toxic foods and prolonged feelings of stress can have harmful, long-term effects on the body. There is too much information to explore on this concept in our works here in much more detail aside from elaborating on its significance and through offering more information on our website.

(Authors' Note: For more resources about how to implement healthy, effective exercise routines in your life, along with further resources about how to use and consume the most optimally nutritious foods and products properly, please visit our website, www.TiltingTheBalance.com/HealthIsWealth).

THE EIGHTH FUNDAMENTAL OF SELF-LOVE: MENTAL HEALTH

"You don't have to control your thoughts. You just have to stop letting them control you."
– Dan Millman

Taking care of our mental health is just as (if not more) important as taking care of our physical bodies.

As humans, we experience a vast array of thoughts that lead us to feel all sorts of varying emotions on a broad spectrum. We know that our thoughts and feelings can be both rational or irrational, and that how we feel is not always permanent. We are no longer living in the same time of fight or flight in the way we were when we were living in the wild and being chased by predators. Even animals living in the wild who are being hunted today have adapted with the ability to shake off fear and trauma. Although they may perceive these as traumatic events, they have learned how to quickly continue onwards, so that they do not become more easily susceptible as prey for the next animal that comes along.

We tend to hold onto traumas we have experienced in our lives, and the circumstances that may have caused our individual traumas can be widely subjective. What one of us may experience and hold to be insignificant can sometimes be perceived as a significant traumatic event for someone else, or vice versa. Living in a state of fear or trauma can be detrimental to the cultivation of the positive futures we may desire for ourselves. Ultimately, we are still living in a state of survival, either working to escape the threats of taking care of our bodies, our environments, or of time itself. We are no different than the animals in the wild though in the sense that we must understand how to stay alert, self-aware, and in the present moment.

When we are residing in feelings of fear or trauma, we can often overlook or even sabotage options, opportunities, or outcomes that could possibly affect our lives in positive ways. This supports why we must identify our existing traumas and fears so that we can discover and implement the best strategies for how to overcome or relinquish them, and uncover and utilize the best practices that will develop our resilience to prevent ourselves from experiencing possible traumas or irrational fears in the future.

We also need to learn how to put ourselves first, to find the balance in being selfish versus selfless, to know our triggers, and to understand what causes us to experience pleasure and pain. Since we tend to make our decisions based on the feelings they will result in and with the thoughts of how our actions will cause us to experience subsequent levels of pleasure versus pain, we need to identify powerful reasons for why we want to take directive action to enable us to stay committed to the processes of creating changes.

In addition, we must understand that how we treat our mental health can directly impact our physical health. Where the mind goes, the body follows, and there is scientific research that supports how chemicals that are released in our bodies when we experience continued stress can negatively impact our physical conditions.

Essentially, when we allow ourselves to place our energy and focus on issues in our external environment, we leave little energy for our bodies to take care of our internal environment. This is why it is so crucial for us as humans to learn healthy coping skills to aid us in overcoming the stresses, traumas, and fears that life presents to us. We must learn healthy ways to reduce our stress, release our negative emotional attachments, find laughter and humor, effectively and appropriately communicate through our problems, identify and create solutions, and experience more positive overall thoughts and feelings.

Even with addictions, we must realize that the root cause of them is associated with some memorized emotion that is guiding the behaviors, and that our addictions both create our habits and help shape our personalities, identities, and our overall self-image.

This is where mental health therapies can become so beneficial in overcoming many of our mental afflictions.

You will find that we delve further into the benefits of mental health therapies as you continue reading this book.

Here is an excerpt from "*Chapter 5: Physical Fitness & Mental Wellness*" which you will read later in this book:

"*On the topic of mental health, there is a massive stigma associated with seeking mental health therapy. You do not have to share your struggles with the world but holding these struggles inward can cause more serious issues, ranging from mental and physical illnesses all the way to death. There are many benefits associated with seeking mental health therapy from qualified professionals and discussing your internal feelings with someone who is trained to unbiasedly listen and help guide you.*"

Not only can direct mental health therapy and various forms of psychotherapies have positive effects on our minds, but they can also improve our psyche, and our overall state of well-being. There are also numerous mental health exercises and techniques that can be performed and utilized to help promote a more positive life for ourselves.

We can make use of journals or enlist the direct services of mental health professionals (both of which are super powerful, evidence-based, and we highly recommend), and there are also exercises and techniques ranging from Neuro-Linguistic Programming, Hypnotherapy, Homeopathy, Acupuncture, Massage Therapy, Music Therapy, Aromatherapy, Herbal Medicine, Yoga, Martial Arts, Anchoring, Spiritual/Energy/Emotional Therapy, and much more. There are also, as we already mentioned of course, affirmation, meditation, visualization, and gratitude practices which are all readily available. Even participating in activities from your favorite hobbies, passions, and interests can serve as forms of mental health therapies.

No matter what avenues you choose to explore, it is imperative that you find what types of mental health therapies best work for you.

(Authors' Note: We can change our realities by changing our mindsets and the ways we think, feel, emote, and act. Be sure to check out our resources that can help with your mental health and overall well-being by visiting our website at www.TiltingTheBalance.com/HealthIsWealth.

In addition, you can schedule a direct one-on-one coaching session or see what other exciting offers we currently have available by visiting www.TiltingTheBalance.com/LiveLearning).

THE NINTH FUNDAMENTAL OF SELF-LOVE: SOCIAL INFLUENCE

"Leadership is influence."
– John C. Maxwell

In regards to John C. Maxwell's quote, the questions are, who are you following, and, who are you influencing?

Psychology suggests that social influence is the process by which an individual is impacted and modified by the presence or actions of others.

This is why in regards to "Social Influence" as part of "*The 10 Fundamentals of Self- Love,*" we are referring to others who are both directly and indirectly part of your life and how their thoughts, feelings, emotions, attitudes, behaviors, actions, decisions, indecisions, reactions, perspectives, influences, habits, paradigms, and other potential variables may affect and impact you.

Ask yourself, how are those who are the most influential to you making an impact on those around them? Are they contributing in positive ways: educating, inspiring, encouraging, entertaining, supporting, and uplifting others? Or are they contributing negatively: belittling, begrudging, discouraging, or judging others or being vindictive?

Although there is an exorbitant amount of additional traits we could mention for both ends of the spectrum, the biggest question to consider is whether or not your influences are overall more optimistic, altruistic, or selfless or if they are rather more pessimistic, uncompromising, or selfish in their nature.

It is crucial to have the right social influences in your world. Whether you may notice it or not, other people around you can have a direct impact on who you are, what you think, and how you act. This can include people who you directly spend time with in your life (your friends, family, romantic partners), people who you watch on television or follow on social media, those whose ideas you read in books, magazines, articles, or other publications, to information you may receive through various communications, syndications, broadcasts, or even from those who individually or institutionally impose rules which you may or may not opt to follow.

It is known that experience can modify social and emotional behavior. There is also much evidence to support that when we experience stress, trauma, or adversity, especially at early stages in life, it can result in lasting alterations of our behavior. Today, neuroscientists are rigorously testing how various forms of mental training can bring about strong and lasting effects on our behaviors. What we do know is that our brains can be rewired to function in new ways from how they may have previously functioned through a process known as neuroplasticity, also referred to as brain or neural plasticity. It is how our brains change through growth and reorganization via the ability of neural networks in the brain.

Social influences can very well have an effect on these processes. We have what are called "mirror neurons," which are a type of brain cell that responds equally when we perform an action and, fascinatingly, when someone else performs the same action. This means other peoples' emotions can physically become contagious and affect our own, and is why it is so important to abstain from social influences that can lead to unfavorable or negative escalating emotions.

(Authors' Note: This is directly from Transformation Academy's "Emotional Intelligence Life Coach Course": So, how powerful is this influence? In 2000, the journal Psychological Science published a study in which participants were shown a face with either a happy, angry, or neutral expression. They were shown the image for only 30 milliseconds, so they were not consciously aware of what expression they were being exposed to. Their unconscious minds picked up the image, and when they were shown images displaying happiness, their bodies reacted by increasing electrical activity in the muscles needed to smile. The same thing happened for those who were exposed to images of anger. What is powerful is that participants were seeing the images for just 30 milliseconds, and their bodies were reacting automatically, even though they were completely unaware that they had seen this image. Now, imagine the impact that the people around you who are expressing a strong emotional state can have on your body's reaction! Another study that was published in the journal PLOS One found that we are also influenced by observing another person experiencing physical sensations. In the study, they showed participants video of a hand that was placed into either visibly cold or visibly warm water. The study found that the participants' hand temperatures actually changed based on what they saw in the video. For example, when a video was shown of someone putting their hand in cold water, the participant's hand dropped in temperature.

These studies, among many others, truly demonstrate that those around us can influence us at a deep level. We highly recommend Transformation Academy's platform for obtaining coaching certifications and expanding your personal development. Visit www.TiltingTheBalance.com/TransformationAcademy to learn more).

The reality of it is, all of us have social influences, and some can be changed and modified where others may or cannot. We understand you may be in a position where you cannot easily change all of your social variables. However, you do have the power to always change your very mindset, and that is one of the most vital fundamental principles in life for you to understand.

We highly recommend you spend the most time affiliating yourself with people who are making positive differences in this world. These are the people who should be influencing you, whose works you should be watching, reading, and listening to, and whose leadership you should be following.

You can also become a leader, and this is a strong reason to support the power of being creative. When we are in creative states, we can disassociate from our known realities. We can unplug from others, our belongings, our tasks, our pasts, our futures, and even ourselves.

We encourage you to become the creator of everything you want and aspire toward. In doing so, simultaneously strive toward being a positive social influence to those around you by surrounding yourself with other positive leaders, and through emulating those leaders in your thoughts, feelings, emotions, and actions.

(Authors' Note: Social influence is one of the most powerful forces shaping your mindset, decisions, and direction in life. The people we surround ourselves with, the content we consume, and the behaviors we witness collectively affect us more than we may realize. This is why we must become more aware and intentional about who and what we allow to influence us.

Start by taking inventory of your current social ecosystem. Reflect on who energizes and who drains you. Consider what kind of content you engage with on a daily basis and how it regularly impacts your thoughts, feelings, self-image, beliefs, and focus. In your audits, be mindful that where all influence may not immediately be visible to the conscious mind, it is always active. Our brains are wired to mirror behaviors and emotional signals from those around us, which means social input has the power to physically and mentally rewire the ways we think and feel.

This supports why, next, you want to begin designing your environment with purpose. Choose your social inputs and relationships with great care. While we will explore how to create healthy boundaries in the next fundamental, it starts by recognizing what influences need to shift. Pay attention to the people and messages that shape your inner world and make space for better ones to enter. Consider seeking out aligned communities, whether they are in person or virtual, where growth, personal responsibility, and inspiration are a shared and constant focus.

You can also begin immediately cultivating high-value relationships by practicing the reciprocity principle. Become the kind of person you want to attract. Communicate with clarity, lead with service and integrity, and build strong partnerships that support both the growth of others and yourself.

Napoleon Hill reviewed the power of mastermind groups such as these in his classic Think and Grow Rich. They are a tremendous way to connect with others through a combination of brainstorming, education, peer accountability, and support to help improve both your personal and professional skills. The reality is, your environment can either pull you backward or propel you forward. The beauty lies in your ability to choose the direction.

As you continue, do so with purpose, remembering that you are not just being influenced, but that you are also actively influencing others. You have the choice to lead by example, which could ultimately encourage, inspire, motivate, and uplift those around you. Adversely, you can choose to perpetuate the negativity that is already far too common in our world today. Our environment is not just something we inherit; it is something we create. It is up to you. This all supports exactly why we each have an individual responsibility to be the change we want to see in the world).

THE TENTH FUNDAMENTAL OF SELF-LOVE: ROUTINES & BOUNDARIES

"You don't have to be great to start, but you have to start to be great."
— Zig Ziglar

A routine is a fixed program and sequence of regularly followed and performed actions. They can also be referred to as rituals. However, what does this have to do with self-love?

The answer? Everything!

You see, it all begins with habits. Allow us to explain. Merriam-Webster's Dictionary defines a habit as, *"a usual way of behaving: something that a person does often in a regular and repeated way."*

Take a moment to think of the many egregious habits that people have. You may even struggle with some of them yourself. People will smoke, consume alcohol or drugs, bite their fingernails, binge watch television, excessively gamble, overeat food, and partake in all sorts of negative and/or detrimental activities. Negative and destructive types of habits take time to form and to become routines in peoples' lives. Just as they take time to form, they take time to unform just the same. Everything takes time, and this is yet another vital fundamental life principle to understand. You will see that we will touch upon these principles several times as you continue reading forward.

As Co-Author Nick Houpt often quotes, *"When it comes down to it, everything in your life is based on your decisions and choices."*

Research suggests that it can take eighteen to two hundred and fifty-four days for a new habit to form and that it takes an average of around sixty-six days in order for a new behavior to become automatic. It is not just about the length of time that dictates how long it takes to form new habits or to modify existing ones. It is also about repetition related to the development of new habits, meaning how many times you repeat new specific actions. As you continue forward into the additional *"10 Categories of Life,"* we encourage you to consider how you can create routines and set goals that will aid you in implementing better habits.

Merriam-Webster's Dictionary defines a routine as, *"a regular course of procedure."* This is why you want to create routines for yourself, as it will create a series of actions with an ongoing timeline paralleled with the time it takes for a new habit to form and for old ones to be eliminated and replaced. This is a critical element in understanding how to transform your habits; knowing that your habits are not unlearned but rather that they are replaced with new ones. You must create and implement routines for yourself that support the development of new habits. These new habits will replace those which are not giving you the desired outcomes you want and will help lead to the outcomes to which you aspire. The creation of new habits will begin to shift your paradigms, which encompass your standards, perspectives, and sets of ideas and your overall viewpoints of yourself and of the world around you. Changing your habits will change your usual ways of thinking about things or how you do them since you will be replacing them in new and different ways. This is so powerful because, as we have reviewed several times now, when you begin to change your thinking, you can begin to change your life.

(Authors' Note: Willpower is our ability to delay gratification and resist our short-term temptations. It also aids us in meeting our long-term goals. However, research suggests that we only have so much willpower on a daily basis. This supports why it is more advantageous for us to focus on changing our habits when it comes to making lasting changes. You can fast-track your habit transformation process as well by learning how to make it easy to change your habits and becoming aware of how to modify your habit loops. Habit loops are the framework for how and why habits are developed through a three-step process with associated cues, routines, and rewards. Cues trigger the development of our habitual behaviors, routines become the habitual behaviors themselves, and the reward is how our brains believe the behaviors positively benefit us. We suggest reading Atomic Habits by James Clear to learn some amazing systems such as habit stacking and other ways for how to most effectively change your habits. You can find it by visiting www.TiltingTheBalance.com/OurFavoriteBooks).

In the modern world at the time this book was published, the vast power of technology makes us all much more connected with others than ever before in history. Unless there is a major dark age again, this phenomenon will only continue to progress. Where there are a tremendous amount of benefits to this newfound power, there are also a multitude of unfavorable associated consequences.

It can be a massive struggle to disconnect from the world and most importantly, from the agendas for your life imposed by others, especially through the power of technology. Renowned brain and memory coach, Jim Kwik, said it best in one of Be Inspired's YouTube videos titled, *"You Will Never Be Lazy Again | Jim Kwik"*: *"My friend Brendon Burchard says, 'An inbox is nothing but a convenient organizational system for other people's agenda for your life.'"*

This is profoundly (and sadly) accurate... Mail, email, phone calls, text messages, instant messages, direct messages, you name it; when we receive and open these communications, we are most often (though not always of course) being reactive in these instances to other individuals' or organizations' wills as opposed to being proactive with our own.

You see, this is why creating routines and setting times where you are proactive on your own agenda has everything to do with taking care of yourself and practicing self-love. You must make time to do the things required for yourself, unobstructed by everyone else's agenda for your life. This is also why we recommend turning off all your electronic device notifications to help eliminate these distractions.

When we implement routines for ourselves, not only are we spending valuable time (which is critical for ourselves as separate individuals), but we are also performing greater miracles in neuroscience within our very own minds which will help wire our brains for success.

The bottom line is that you need your own unobstructed and undisturbed personal time each and every day to perform the necessary actions that are required to attain both your physical and mental goals. This is why we strongly encourage you to learn and understand the practice of hard scheduling your time (known also as time blocking or timeboxing) as well as understanding the art and power of focus.

(Authors' Note: For more details on how to most effectively implement the practice of hard scheduling in your life, please visit www.TiltingTheBalance.com/HardScheduling).

What you focus on expands. As we reviewed in the beginning of this book, our very concept of "tilting the balance" is the understanding that everything in life is all about compounding interest through our collective thoughts and actions (or inactions) over the course of time. Creating and living by routines in your life is an unquestionably powerful way to implement all of the teachings and principles throughout this book and is in our opinion the second most effective way to hit your goals and to achieve your dreams. The first most powerful way, you might ask? To take massive, focused, directive action, of course, which you are already doing by reading and getting to this point in our book.

Part of the reason routines are so effective is due to the power of procedural memories, a type of implicit memory. Procedural memories aid us in the performance of tasks we perform, and frequently without any need for our conscious levels of awareness. Essentially, when we have routines, we help create these memories and form habit loops that help us get things done without us needing to consciously think about it. We can implement routines to help us create habits in all areas of our lives. We can form exercise routines, meal planning routines, routines of completing personal tasks, contacting or spending time with specific individuals, taking our significant others on dates, meditating, visualizing, citing affirmations, performing gratitude techniques, and create routines for just about everything within "*The 10 Fundamentals of Self-Love*" and "*The 10 Categories of Life.*"

You see, you can create patterns of behaviors that will help you get to where you want to go in all areas of your life.

(Authors' Note: We highly recommend reading Hal Elrod's The Miracle Morning: The Not-So-Obvious Secret Guaranteed to Transform Your Life (Before 8AM). He gives some wonderful strategies on ways to structure a routine and provides a copious amount of insight relative to their power. We also recommend The 5 Second Rule: Transform your Life, Work, and Confidence with Everyday Courage by Mel Robbins, to learn about the power of getting into the routine of using five second countdowns that can help prompt us in taking more massive action. To find these books and all of the others we recommend available for purchase, visit www.TiltingTheBalance.com/OurFavoriteBooks).

We also encourage you to get in the routine of creating and implementing effective boundaries. Boundaries are rules, limitations, and guidelines that we individually set forth that direct how we want to be treated, dictate what we do and do not find acceptable, and sets clear expectations as to what we are willing and unwilling to tolerate. They help keep us feeling safe, respected, and are an integral aspect of demonstrating self-love.

We can create physical, mental, and emotional boundaries, sexual boundaries, time boundaries, religious, spiritual, materialistic, financial, and non-negotiable boundaries. We can also create intrapersonal boundaries and implement them through interpersonal relationships with family, friends, our romantic partners, business partners, colleagues, associates, and even with strangers. These boundaries establish agreements that set proper expectations for how others must appropriately interact with us, and we can enforce boundaries with ourselves, imposing rules, limitations, and guidelines for our own actions.

Through setting effective boundaries, we can:
- Ensure our individual needs are met
- Gain clarity on our values, belief systems, who we are, and what we want
- Stay true to ourselves, our values, beliefs, desires, and goals
- Increase our self-respect and develop more respect both from and for others
- Develop a greater sense of our compassion, independence, identity, self-image, and self-esteem
- Enhance our inner peace, security, assertiveness, and our overall physical, mental, emotional, and spiritual well-being
- Increase our time, energy, self-awareness, and positive feelings
- Decrease future drama, conflicts, and feelings of guilt, stress, anger, resentment, or burnout
- More easily overcome negative relationships, addictions, dependency issues, rejection
- & much more!

The goal is to set reasonable consequences with both others and with ourselves when our boundaries are violated. So, how exactly do we set proper boundaries?

One of the most effective ways is to communicate them, to express our feelings when they are being crossed, or to appropriately convey them before they are. We can walk away from people in the moment, distance ourselves from them for extended periods of time, or even remove them from our lives entirely. We can also ask for intermediaries to get involved, from seeking professional counselors to help us better communicate with loved ones, utilizing human resource managers for workplace issues, to seeking bouncers at a bar to intervene when a patron is overly inebriated or aggressive.

As extreme as it may sound, physical violence can even be a boundary, though it should most likely only be exercised when your life or someone else's may be endangered. It is important to keep in mind that legal ramifications can be associated with opting to physically touch someone, even during instances where you may be defending yourself or others.

The bottom line is, boundaries are essentially emotional self-defense strategies. We have to determine when and where to create boundaries on our own, if or when we need assistance enforcing boundaries, and to what degree we opt to enforce them. Sometimes, we also need to decide when implementing boundaries may be a losing battle to where we must completely remove ourselves from certain people, circumstances, scenarios, or situations.

Again, you are individually responsible for your own happiness. Unless you are being compensated or are providing a direct service, it is typically not your role to please others or to make them happy.

You must understand, the word 'no' can be a complete sentence, and if you want to become a master of creating your desired reality, you must learn to become a master of creating and implementing boundaries. This does not mean you cannot still effectively listen to and seek other points of view while simultaneously respecting your own. This also does not mean you do not have the right to change your mind, preferences, or positions.

Having and enforcing ethical boundaries will grant you with the ability to be authentic and true to yourself, to others, and will allow you the ability to prioritize time for self-love and care, free of guilt, disrespect, distractions, or interruptions.

As far as getting started, the first step is to become self-aware of how and why each boundary is important to you, and how and why they will benefit your life and well-being. Once you have done your self-reflection, the next steps are to create the framework for your boundaries and then implement them. You may want to start small and at your own pace, so that you can become comfortable utilizing them in order to remain consistent. Boundaries are all about self-worth, self-value, and self-care.

Here are some ways you can begin applying them in your life for both yourself and with others:
- Communicating your direct needs, feelings, positions, and expectations
- Communicating how others' behaviors and actions may be negatively impacting you or others, how it makes you feel, and what the consequences will be if they continue
- Limiting or eliminating communications with specific individuals or setting time frames where you are unavailable to communicate in general
- Refusing to participate in specific discussions, activities, or conflicts
- Admitting when you are at fault and knowing when to deny blame
- Giving and receiving help, respect, and/or space to both yourself and others
- Setting parameters where you or others are allowed or not allowed to have specific discussions or perform specific activities
- Limiting the allotment of your time, money, or resources to others or even yourself

Where these are general principles, here are several specific examples that may help shed some insight on how you can apply them:
- Not working, taking calls, checking emails, setting meetings, etc. on certain days or at certain times to allow yourself space or time to decompress, to tend to self-care needs, or manage other personal affairs
- Limiting or eliminating financial spending, time spent watching television, playing video games, on social media, etc.
- Sharing with others what topics you will not discuss, activities you will not participate in, or what behaviors you will not accept or appreciate
- Communicating with romantic partners your sexual needs and turn-offs
- Choosing what resources you have that you are open to sharing and with whom you are open to sharing those resources with

While these are just examples, this content is so comprehensive, it could fill another book in itself. You must always bear in mind that others have their own individual boundaries as well, and by having your own, it can help create more mutual empathy and respect in your relationships with others, and better the internal relationship you have with yourself. We all have our rights to our own time, to express our needs, avoid negativity, have personal privacy, to stand-up for ourselves and others, and to respect ourselves and our beliefs. Where it takes a great deal of inner confidence and self-security, setting and enforcing boundaries is extremely self-empowering. We encourage you to learn as much as you can about how to most effectively implement them into your life.

Now that you are familiar with *"The 10 Fundamentals of Self-Love,"* we want you to keep in mind how they relate and align with your life, goals, dreams, and desires as you progress forward in understanding *"The 10 Categories of Life,"* which we will begin reviewing next. Make sure that you are always thinking about how all of these fundamentals integrate and correspond with your perspective goals and actions as you continue to read on.

CHAPTER 3
PERSONAL TASKS

"I long to accomplish a great and noble task, but it is my chief duty to accomplish small tasks as if they were great and noble."
– Helen Keller

All of us have personal tasks that must be accomplished. Some are big, some are small, some are one-time events while others are more recurring. These tasks could include washing your car, doing your dishes or laundry, finishing a passion-project, paying your bills, filing your taxes, obtaining or renewing passports or licenses, and decorating your living space. There are numerous examples of personal tasks we may have to complete in our lives.

Have you ever completed a small task that you had really been wanting or urging to get done? How did it make you feel? When we complete a task, it usually makes us feel pretty great. This is why we chose to start with personal tasks in this book. Understand, we are not saying you must complete each and every one of your tasks before you can move on, as we understand some tasks will get done more quickly while others may need time to accomplish along the way. This is more about identifying all of them as a collective whole.

As it relates to your personal tasks, we also urge you to ponder which of them can be outsourced, delegated, or automated. For example, is hiring a cleaning company, a dry-cleaner, a mobile car detailing service, a nanny, a pet sitter or groomer, a landscaper, virtual assistant, or any other service provider an option to allow you more free time? If so, it can also become a personal task to find, interview, and hire these providers for their services. In addition to thinking through those factors, this is also a place to think about other ways in which you can be more efficient at accomplishing your personal tasks. Can you utilize artificial intelligence or time management automation technologies, find ways to read and expand your knowledge of useful strategies in these areas, or even enlist the services of specialized mentors or coaches? Are there ways you can double-up on your tasks? For example, doing dishes, cleaning up, or organizing your personal spaces while you do laundry? Are there areas in your schedule where you may have something on the agenda but there might be some downtime within it where you can accomplish some of your personal tasks? The key here is to think about how you can be the most efficient.

Getting a strong grip over your personal tasks and completing a few of your smaller goals in these areas will immediately help progress you toward shortening your long list of goals and desires from your *"Mind Dump."* It will also help you to begin building positive momentum toward feeling good about being able to set and accomplish some of your goals. Prioritizing and completing these types of goals is also essential to streamlining your processes. As our great friend Grayson Marshall, Jr., an ACC Legend and hall of fame and Clemson basketball player, published author, motivational speaker, and successful life coach says, "There is no conflict in priority."

(Authors' Note: In the book, Make Your Bed: Little Things That Can Change Your Life... and Maybe the World, written by retired Admiral William H. Mcraven, U.S. Navy Sea, Air, and Land (SEAL), and former commander of Joint Special Operations Command, Mcraven explains in detail ten life lessons he learned through his experiences in his military career.

As stated in his commencement speech at the University of Texas: "If you want to change the world, start off by making your bed. If you make your bed every morning, you will have accomplished the first task of the day. It will give you a small sense of pride, and it will encourage you to do another task, and another, and another. And by the end of the day that one task completed will have turned into many tasks completed."

Therefore, making your bed is an excellent practice to consider implementing as part of your daily routine. You can find this book, and Hal Elrod's The Miracle Morning: The Not-So-Obvious Secret Guaranteed to Transform Your Life (Before 8AM) which we also recommend for helping with some of your personal tasks, and more by visiting www.TiltingTheBalance.com/OurFavoriteBooks).

In this section, we want you to identify and take all of the personal tasks and responsibilities from your "Mind Dump" and organize them into your recurring and nonrecurring tasks.

Here is how to set it up within your template:

ITEM/GOAL	TIME FRAME	PRIORITY
Write down all of your Personal Tasks	How often do you want to do each task? (e.g. 1 time, "x" times, weekly/monthly/quarterly/semiannually/annually/biennially)	Rate tasks on a priority scale from Low, Medium, to High

(Authors' Note: If you do not wish to write in your copy of this book, or if you need a fresh template, please feel free to download this template separately by visiting www.TiltingTheBalance.com/Templates).

Once you have written down your goal or item, your time frame for that goal, and the priority level it is to you, you will move on to the next section of the template. In this section of the template, you will write down how you feel in this area, whether those are feelings about yourself or about the items or goals specifically. This is very important to think about as we stated earlier in "The Self, Core Values, & Belief Systems" chapter. Do not worry if some of these feelings are negative because we are going to work through them as we progress further along. Some examples for this specific category may be:

Today, in this category I feel:
- Overwhelmed with all of my clutter and stressed out because I have too much to do
- I can actually afford to hire some help
- I am not a very organized person
- Happy that I am moving forward to make these changes

In the template, you can use the bullet point format, you can write your feelings out as complete sentences or just simple words; whatever works best for you.

Once you have finished that portion, you will move on to writing what you feel are factors or beliefs holding you back in each category. These can consist of thoughts, feelings, or beliefs such as those presented in the next example.

These are the factors or beliefs that are holding me back in this category:
- I do not have the time to accomplish (specific goal or item)
- My family is a priority over (specific goal or item)
- I do not believe I deserve this (specific goal or item)
- I'm not skilled enough to get this (specific goal or item) done

Whatever you think is holding you back, write it all down. After you complete that section, you will then move on to the area where you focus on implementing boundaries and/or routines. Here are some examples.

These are the boundaries and/or routines I need to implement and enforce:
- I need to limit or eliminate my time spent (in a specific area or doing specific things) to allow me more time to accomplish (specific goal or item)
- I need to figure out how to not allow (specific thing) to take precedence over spending the time I want to with my family
- I need to do (specific action, such as affirmations as an example) to reinforce the belief that I do in fact deserve (specific goal or item)
- I need to find a way to dedicate time to do (specific task) to learn and acquire the skills I need to get this (specific goal or item) done or to find someone who can help me

Next, we move to focusing on the positives to start transforming those negative and self-limiting beliefs. This is where you will start to think about what you are grateful for. As we said, we all have things to be grateful for, whether we know it or not. Take the time to focus and write down what you are grateful for in this present moment. Some examples are:

Today I am grateful for:
- I am grateful for waking up today
- I am grateful for my family
- I am grateful for (specific resource or material possession)
- I am grateful that I can see, read, learn, walk, talk, touch, feel, laugh, etc.

The goal is to write down whatever positive thoughts that may come to mind.

Once you have completed focusing on gratitude, it is time to move on to writing down your affirmations. This is where you will flip any of those negative beliefs, thoughts, or feelings you may have written into more positive and beneficial beliefs, thoughts, and feelings. If you need a refresher on how to most effectively write out your affirmations, please revisit the "affirmations" section in "The Self, Core Values, & Belief Systems" chapter.

Using examples from the ones above, your goal is to take those negative statements and turn them into definite, positive affirmations. They will look something like this:

Original statement: I feel overwhelmed with all of my clutter and stressed out because I have too much to do.
New affirmation: I am always feeling calm, always organized, and always have plenty of time to do what I need to do.

Original statement: I am not an organized person.
New affirmation: I am always an organized person.

Original statement: I do not have the time to accomplish (specific goal or item).
New affirmation: I always have the time to accomplish what needs to be done.

Original statement: I do not believe I deserve this (specific goal or item).
New affirmation: I am always worthy and deserving of the things I desire.

You see, the goal is to take the negative statement and affirm the exact opposite. As you accomplish each template, the goal is to create a routine of focusing on the items you wrote down for which you are grateful, along with your affirmations, to help you reframe your perspective and begin creating a more positive belief system about yourself and your life.

This is how you will fill out your templates for each category in "*The 10 Categories of Life*" chapters. Please feel free to revisit this if you need to do so, should you need help completing your templates as you go along.

(Authors' Note: We provide in-depth, direct one-on-one coaching services if you feel you need guidance completing these templates and formulating corrective action. To learn more about our current offers, please visit www.TiltingTheBalance.com/LiveLearning).

We urge you not to concern yourself so much with immediate deadlines at this time unless an item *must absolutely* be done in a certain allotted time frame. When you apply the pressure of time with all of your collective goals, it can often create unwanted anxiety and stress, which does not aid you in positive thinking nor help get you much closer to accomplishing them. Formatting your goals in this way initially will allow you to clearly see your goals written in front of you in an organized fashion; an important early step to goal success.

We are going to revisit all of your goals after we review all of *"The 10 Categories of Life"* and we will teach you how to use the *"S.M.A.R.T. Goal"* formula to help you further organize your goals, their priority levels, and their time frames so that you can take them to the highest level of achievement possible.

(Authors' Note: As mentioned prior, we encourage you to read Think and Grow Rich by Napoleon Hill along with The Secret by Rhonda Byrne to better understand how to apply the Law of Attraction in your life. These works highlight why it is essential to think positively, reduce stress, and maintain belief in your vision, all of which plays a crucial role in helping you accomplish your dreams. Positive thinking and emotional alignment are just as important for handling day-to-day tasks as they are for bringing long-term goals to life. For further reading on this subject matter, we also recommend The Divine Matrix by Gregg Braden and The Master Key System by Charles F. Haanel.

Another key to goal success is understanding how your habits shape your thinking. When you learn how to adjust your habits intentionally, you begin to optimize your time, energy, and results. To explore this concept further, visit www.TiltingTheBalance.com/KeystoneHabits to learn more about the power of keystone habits).

You are now ready to complete your own *"Personal Tasks"* template.

PERSONAL TASKS		
Item/Goal	Time Frame	Priority Level

Item/Goal	Time Frame	Priority Level

Today, in this category, I feel:

These factors or beliefs are holding me back in this category:

PERSONAL TASKS

These are the boundaries and/or routines I need to implement and enforce:

Today, I am grateful for:

These are the most beneficial affirmations for me in this category:

CHAPTER 4
PHYSICAL FITNESS & MENTAL WELLNESS

"Physical exercise improves health, mental exercise improves wealth, laziness destroys both."
– Bruce Lee

Now that you have organized all of your personal tasks, it is time to move on to your physical and mental health. There is an abundance of science and data to support the imperativeness of living a both physically and mentally healthy lifestyle. A healthy mind, body, and spirit help to encourage positive thinking and an overall more positive and confident outlook on life. It affects the way we see ourselves internally, externally, and impacts how both we and others may view our internal and external selves.

Here we encourage you to consider goals such as cooking for yourself or meal planning; formulating and practicing a weight resistance routine; losing or gaining weight; implementing stretching, cardio, calisthenics, yoga, walking, biking, martial arts, or other fitness regimens; and even seeking out mental health counseling. You can contemplate hiring personal trainers, fitness, wellness, or accountability coaches, dietitians, nutritionists, or any specialists who can aid you with implementing proper health, nutrition, and exercise techniques and routines. You can also read books and take various actions to further educate yourself to expand your knowledge in these areas.

Additionally, this is the space to consider whether or not you may need to see other medical providers for routine examinations; to schedule a necessary medical procedure; refill, retake, or relinquish certain medications and prescribed activities.

Here, we also encourage you to reflect on goals based around getting the most optimal amount of sleep your body requires, as well as getting the proper amount of water and nutritional needs your body must have on a continual basis. When you are living a healthy lifestyle and implementing healthy routines, it will positively impact your mindset and appearance, which comes with its many benefits and will boost your personal confidence in both yourself and in your abilities.

This is also an area where we encourage you to draw awareness of any addictions or unhealthy coping mechanisms that may be negatively impacting your life. It is critical to understand how these dynamics may be affecting both your physical and mental health.

On the topic of mental health, there is a massive stigma associated with seeking mental health therapy. You do not have to share your struggles with the world, but holding these struggles inward can cause more serious issues, ranging from mental and physical illnesses all the way to death. There are many benefits associated with seeking mental health therapy from qualified professionals and discussing your internal feelings with someone who is professionally trained to unbiasedly listen and guide you.

Aside from therapy and guidance, there are plenty of tasks that can improve your mental well-being. Not only are there many mental health exercises you can do, some of which we reviewed in *"The 10 Fundamentals of Self-Love,"* ranging from reciting affirmations, meditating, visualizing, writing down things for which you are grateful, and following routines, there are also numerous activities you can do which will all fall into different areas under *"The 10 Categories of Life."*

Completing personal tasks can aid your mental health. You can enjoy spending time with family, friends, or a romantic partner, or taking and setting aside some personal time for yourself. You can spend time enjoying some of your hobbies, passions, and interests, working in or on your business, or even making time to volunteer. All of these activities can have a beneficial impact on our mental health. However, as yet another one of life's curious juxtapositions, spending too little or too much time in these areas that are meaningful for us can have negative consequences in our lives just the same.

You see, it all depends on exactly what it is we want and how much of a priority it is to attain our wants that should determine how we each individually choose to spend our time "tilting the balance" in our lives. Doing positive, productive, and healthy things that make us feel good are exactly the actions we want to take so that we may attain a strong and sustainable state of mental health, physical health, and overall well-being.

Sometimes though, we must take action doing things we have little-to-no desire to do so that the consequences of not doing them will not weigh out negatively in our lives.

Ensuring that we are balancing the ways we spend our time in all of the areas in our lives is the primary key to our physical and mental health, as well as to our success overall. To every benefit, comes a consequence. That is the game of life in its own essence: learning how to weigh out, prioritize, and effectively execute every decision we make so that we may live the most smooth, happy, healthy, successful, and fulfilled lives we possibly can.

This leads us to another significant aspect about our lives as it relates to our overall sense of well-being which we briefly mentioned earlier (and will again). It is the very concept of time. As author and accomplished entrepreneur Harvey Brown (also Justin's grandfather) puts it, "An axiom by which we should all live by is that time is the most important and valuable asset we have. Without time, there is no wealth, health, materials, or anything else for that matter."

Most ultimately, our time is the greatest gift we have in our lives, and our lives and legacies are all built upon exactly how we choose to use it. This book is designed to help you set, prioritize, and achieve your goals by helping you understand precisely where and how you need to spend your time. This is what we believe is the greatest power in understanding and mastering the art of "tilting the balance" in your life.

Returning back to mental health, Coach Corey Wayne, successful author and relationship coach, provides a great example in his book titled, *How To Be A 3% Man*. He highlights how when a child falls (and is not seriously injured of course), the child may or may not cry, and will then allow themselves to experience their pain, become present with their emotions; only to let it all go shortly thereafter and continue on with business as usual as if nothing ever happened. As adults, we often tend to mask, hide, or avoid our feelings at times when we are hurt or are faced with positions of vulnerability. Being real, honest, vulnerable, and present with our emotions are not only great steps in overcoming our current pain and trauma, but are also excellent pathways for helping us to avoid them in our future. With these understandings, if you have not already, we encourage you to ignore the stigma surrounding mental health therapy. We encourage you to take proactive steps for improving your mental health and life if you are in an emotionally challenged state due to present or prior negative circumstances and events.

According to the National Alliance on Mental Illness, one in five Americans suffer from a mental illness and, according to the Centers For Disease Control and Prevention, one in twenty-five Americans suffer from serious mental conditions including schizophrenia, major depression, and bipolar disorder. That being said, around sixty percent of people who have mental illnesses do not receive treatment for their conditions.

Seeking professional help to support your mental wellness is an enormous step in improving the overall quality of your life. Living with mental illness may always be a battle in some way. However, receiving the proper guidance or treatment can help make dealing with mental illness much more manageable. Maintaining mental wellness can also positively impact your physical health and productivity in terms of improving your immune system, sleeping habits, focus, and motivation.

Moreover, increased physical fitness has been shown to directly correlate with increased happiness, self-esteem, and energy when performing daily tasks. Your cardiorespiratory endurance is also a determining factor in how active your lifestyle can be. People who have optimal fitness levels have a sheer advantage when it comes to meeting the physical demands of life. When we exercise, we release the neurotransmitter dopamine in the brain and other "feel good" hormones naturally.

This is all based on scientific research. The most common observation made by people who start to physically exercise more often is that they generally feel better and can clearly see an improvement in their wellness, happiness, and functionality. We highly recommend analyzing your current physical fitness activities to observe whether or not you need to make changes to your routines (or to implement one in general) in order to improve your overall health and fitness.

Now it is time to start thinking about your template for this chapter. In the "Time" column, make sure you are realistic. For example, do not write that your goal is to run forty miles daily if you know you most likely will not or cannot do it. However, on the same token, we do not want to discourage you from setting high goals for yourself. (A Wisconsin man named Michael Shattuck averaged running a total of forty miles a day himself and would run sometimes as much as sixty-five hours per week.) We encourage you to hold yourself to a high standard and we only want you to be mindful of your own personal boundaries and obligations when setting goals for yourself. Otherwise, you may risk setting yourself up for becoming discouraged when falling short of set goals, especially those that were likely unachievable from the start. It is highly unlikely that Mr. Shattuck began running at that pace from the very beginning but rather that he was "tilting the balance" in his life, spending time performing the actions he needed to do over the course of time which made it all possible. Setting and attaining goals is all about momentum so, the better you set yourself up in the beginning to take the correct actions which will build that positive momentum, the better your chances are for long-term success.

Keeping your mind in a positive place also makes it easier to take action, especially when we experience these feel-good victories. When we fail repeatedly and set unrealistic goals for ourselves, we make it much harder to keep our minds in a positive place, especially when we continuously experience failures. Not setting significant enough goals though can also set us up for failure as well. If you were not in a position where you wanted things to change, why else might you be continuing to read this book? This then begs the question: why set uninspiring and mediocre goals for yourself?

(Authors' Note: If you do not wish to write in your copy of this book, or if you need a fresh template, please feel free to download this template separately by visiting www.TiltingTheBalance.com/Templates. If you need assistance on how to most effectively complete your template, visit the same hyperlink or you can revisit the detailed instructions in the "Personal Tasks" chapter).

You are now ready to complete your own "Physical Fitness & Mental Wellness" template.

(Authors' Note: If you are experiencing mental turmoil, thoughts of hurting yourself or suicide, emotional distress, or any mental health crisis, please call the 988 Suicide & Crisis Lifeline at 988 or visit 988lifeline.org. The service provides free, confidential support at all hours every day of the week. Remember, you are not alone, there is help available, and you will never know what positive opportunities and experiences may be directly around the corner).

PHYSICAL FITNESS & MENTAL WELLNESS

Item/Goal	Time Frame	Priority Level

Item/Goal	Time Frame	Priority Level

Today, in this category, I feel:

These factors or beliefs are holding me back in this category:

These are the boundaries and/or routines I need to implement and enforce:

Today, I am grateful for:

These are the most beneficial affirmations for me in this category:

CHAPTER 5
HOBBIES, PASSIONS, & INTERESTS

"Doing what you love is the cornerstone of having abundance in your life."
— Dr. Wayne Dyer

Think of each area of your life along with every goal you set as coordinates on a roadmap. Purpose, inspiration, passion, motivation, and focus serve as both your compass and your fuel, guiding you toward conquering your dreams while powering you to reach your desired destinations.

It is imperative that you find your purpose and passions and that you identify what you love in your own life. This helps promote positive thinking, and subsequently, a more positive life for yourself overall. Every one of us has a purpose and some kind of inner passions, whether we have yet to discover them or not. Identifying your own purpose and passions in life is the most meaningful and impactful way to help guide yourself along your journey.

If you already know your purpose and passions in life, then you are already a major step ahead. If not, there is no need to fret, as this section is designed to help get you on the right path.

You will start by pondering these questions: "What is my purpose in life? What are things in my life about which I am passionate?"

(Authors' Note: Where of course there are numerous activities to be (and which should be) enjoyed outside of business, having that core mission of your life's purpose as the major destination on your map is the gateway to your success. This is why having a life mission statement as a guide is so powerful. Simple hobbies, passions, and interests are designed to give you experiences of enjoyment while you work to live out your mission in life, which we all know can oftentimes be a challenge. That is why you must be passionate about your life's purpose and mission and find simple hobbies, passions, and interests to help you so that you can keep going when times get tough. They can also help enhance your purpose.

That is not to say your personal life's mission may or may not enable you to enjoy as many hobbies, passions, and interests as you can whenever you may like. Regardless, it will most likely take time and effort to attain that outcome.

Not only do you want to ponder what areas in life you have passions (which of them bring you the utmost joy, happiness, and fulfillment), you will also need to dive deep to discover the root of your life's meaning and purpose. Essentially, you need to ask why you are here on this earth and what all it is that you seek to accomplish while you are here.

This leads us to the most meaningful nugget we believe we can leave you with in regards to embarking upon this endeavor. Discovering your life's purpose and passions are like planting seeds. It takes time to find the seeds, to plant the seeds, to nourish them, to watch them grow, and to ultimately reap their benefits. When you already have the seeds or are actively in the process of cultivating them, and you know your life's purpose and passions, you are steps ahead of the game. If you do not possess the seeds, you should be grateful to know that you are still steps ahead of most. This seed of thought we wish to plant with you here is the importance of understanding the power associated with knowing your life's purpose and passions. It is liberating, empowering, and imperative, and it is a direct correlation to achieving the overall levels of success you desire from your life).

Having fun, enjoyable, and interesting hobbies aids our mental states by relieving stress, improving our creativity, and can even help to strengthen our relationships with others. Hobbies can serve as an excellent outlet as they can enable us to spend time doing things we personally love and enjoy. Group hobbies are also highly recommended because when we do activities with others, it can boost our own motivation and excitement. It also increases our likelihood of building meaningful and loving connections with new people and can benefit existing relationships if they choose to join us.

Examples of hobbies could include anything from playing an instrument on your own or in a band, recording music, practicing or playing recreational sports, or joining a team or club. They could involve traveling to new destinations, fishing or entering tournaments, watching or making movies, reading or writing books, surfing, kite surfing, rock climbing, knitting, riding powersports, bird watching, gardening, building items, or creating homemade products. Spending time outdoors, in the sun, or simply enjoying fresh air is also among countless other fulfilling possibilities. Not every hobby needs to involve more than one person, so you should look within yourself to figure out what actual activities you may already currently enjoy and what new ones may really excite you. Reading and further educating yourself in this area, in addition to even enlisting the services of a life coach, can also be beneficial if you are struggling to decide what hobbies, passions, or interests to pursue. Always remember, the whole point of having hobbies, passions, and interests is for your own happiness, not for anyone else's.

Another important key point to understand about hobbies, passions, and interests is the fact that there are some activities that may be enjoyable while simultaneously not being the most healthy. Some of these examples may even have associated consequences that can lead to addiction. For example, some individuals may enjoy gambling periodically. Others may pride themselves on being wine connoisseurs, beer enthusiasts, or cigar aficionados. Understand, we are not condoning or condemning this, but recreational drug use is another example of hobbies, passions, and interests for those living in this world we all share. This is why it is so pertinent to abide by *"The 10 Fundamentals of Self-Love"* and to ensure you are always taking the best care of your body, emotions, mind, and spirit.

Many famous and successful people currently have or have had hobbies. Beatles legend John Lennon and former U.S. President Franklin D. Roosevelt both collected stamps; Albert Einstein was an avid sailor (who didn't know how to swim!); author Mark Twain was also an amateur inventor; NBA superstar Tim Duncan not only played basketball but also Dungeons & Dragons; Boxing superstar Mike Tyson races pigeons (yes, you read that right); the list goes on.

This section is where you can have some fun identifying the hobbies, passions, and interests that you currently have or use this space to set goals to explore new hobbies, passions, and interests which you may come to love and enjoy. The possibilities are endless! Whatever you desire to learn or to grow, write it down here in this section.

(Authors' Note: If you do not wish to write in your copy of this book, or if you need a fresh template, please feel free to download this template separately by visiting www.TiltingTheBalance.com/Templates. If you need assistance on how to most effectively complete your template, visit the same hyperlink or you can revisit the detailed instructions in the "Personal Tasks" chapter).

Keep in mind, you may notice that some of your goals fall in line under different chapters and topics. This is okay. It is up to you to decide where you feel they should most appropriately go. It does not hurt to overlap your goals in multiple categories as long as the priority level stays the same for each specific goal.

You are now ready to complete your own *"Hobbies, Passions, & Interests"* template.

HOBBIES, PASSIONS, & INTERESTS

Item/Goal	Time Frame	Priority Level

Item/Goal	Time Frame	Priority Level

Today, in this category, I feel:

These factors or beliefs are holding me back in this category:

These are the boundaries and/or routines I need to implement and enforce:

Today, I am grateful for:

These are the most beneficial affirmations for me in this category:

CHAPTER 6
FAMILY & FRIEND RELATIONSHIPS

"With my experience in life, I want to tell you that having good relationships, compassion and peace of mind is much more important than achievements, awards, degrees or money."
– Sudha Murty

Even if you do not have immediate family, you always have the ability to develop new relationships with people who may become like family. With genealogy research being as vast and accessible as it is today, and it will likely continue to grow, you may also find individuals who are actually members of your family.

Having positive family relationships and friendships is a pertinent aspect of our lives and it is important for us to surround ourselves with family or friends for comfort and stability in times of both joy and stress. Studies show that having strong, healthy relationships with people is a powerful protective factor against mental illness and can help you maintain a high level of mental wellness.

It is also crucial for us to release our emotional attachments for the things in life which do not positively serve us. This is an especially vital principle to abide by as it pertains to how we handle our relationships and dealings with others.

Do you want to cultivate better or more quality relationships with family, friends, or even with new people? It is advised to set aside the time to foster existing relationships you may already cherish and to also spend the time required to establish new connections. If you are seeking to establish new connections, do so with an open and objective mind, operating with the understanding that there is a plethora of amazing people out there.

Keep this point in mind if you do not have many connections or if there are people in your world right now who are not benefiting you positively. It is necessary to always work to surround yourself with happy, loving, emotionally healthy people who have the ability to communicate effectively.

(Nick's Note: When someone pops into my head, I make it a task to contact them as immediately as possible to see how they are doing. This keeps my relationship with that person strong, lets them know that I am thinking of them, and demonstrates the fact that I care. I usually will contact people via a text, phone call, or email).

It is beneficial to have quality, positive, consistent relationships in your life with others. If you have someone in your life who is perpetually contributing to negative interactions, consider how effective communication, mediation, coaching, counseling, or therapy with this person can help solve your issues. If any of those are not possible options, you may need to think about ways you can separate yourself from these individuals, or about how you can let these individual relationships go altogether.

(Authors' Note: Our overall lives and the quality of our relationships have changed drastically since we learned about the art of effective communication. We highly encourage you to read The 7 Habits of Highly Effective People by Stephen Covey to begin learning more about the life-changing concept of how to truly listen, connect, and communicate with others in meaningful, respectful, and productive ways.

Another great resource for building stronger relationships is How to Win Friends and Influence People by Dale Carnegie. You can find these reads and all of our recommended books, as always, at www.TiltingTheBalance.com/OurFavoriteBooks.

It is also extremely beneficial to develop the habit of creating boundaries in your life, not just with others but with yourself as well. Alongside communication and boundaries, understanding and harnessing the power of empathy can significantly enhance your relationships and day-to-day interactions.

Empathy allows us to step outside of our own emotions and see a situation through someone else's perspective. It transforms communication from reaction to understanding, and from conflict to connection. The more we practice it, the more we reduce unnecessary tension and build stronger bonds with those around us. Whether in personal or professional settings, empathy helps us lead with compassion, listen without defensiveness, and resolve issues before they escalate or turn into regret.

As a nominal example, imagine a friend, colleague, or even a perfect stranger overreacting to a situation and snapping at you unexpectedly. Instead of immediately becoming defensive, frustrated, or hurt, empathy gives you the ability to pause your own emotional response and consider what they may be experiencing beyond that single interaction. Perhaps they are overwhelmed with stress or facing personal challenges you are unaware of. That brief moment of perspective can shift your reaction from internalizing their behavior to responding with clarifying questions and care.

Empathy allows you to feel what someone else may be feeling while remaining centered in your own emotions. This not only strengthens your ability to relate to others but also helps you avoid taking things personally in everyday interactions. Developing empathy is a skill, and it is not limited to people. It can extend to animals, other life forms, and even the world around you. Ultimately, it cultivates a deeper sense of awareness, care, and purpose in the way you move through life).

Letting go of relationships can be a difficult challenge, especially if you are "stuck" with someone in a living situation or work scenario where you are unable to avoid someone entirely. In these cases, we encourage you to limit your interactions with these negative individuals as much as possible, especially if they are unwilling to effectively communicate with you.

We reviewed earlier the importance of understanding the gift of your time and why it is necessary to learn how to master your time in order to "tilt the balance" in your life. Based on this, one of the single most pivotal questions you can always ask yourself is what the best use of your time is at any given moment. The key is to appreciate your most valuable possession and asset, which is your time, and to ensure that you do not waste your time on relationships with anything or with anyone that is not cherishing your time or contributing positively to your life. Take massive action to free yourself of any negative relationships or influences with anything or anyone, no matter how difficult this may be. If you are in a negative working environment with an abusive colleague or supervisor, you must not be afraid to contact Human Resources, file grievances with associated governing powers, review your challenges with corporate level officers or directors, seek new employment, or even retain legal counsel if absolutely necessary.

If you are living with a significant other in a toxic environment, you must work to effectively communicate through your challenges, engage in family or couples counseling, or work to cut ties altogether, even if you are financially dependent upon them. There are ways to make this possible. These same principles can apply to any shared living situation, including those with family members, friends, or others you may cohabitate with.

Remember, not all relationships are beneficial for us, and in most instances, we are in full control of what we choose to allow and tolerate from others in our lives. Our relationships can either help or destroy our well-being. We cannot always choose the people with whom we have relationships, but if they are negative or toxic, we can choose to limit our interactions or the time spent with these individuals.

Referencing our friend Grayson Marshall, Jr. again, "You must not fall in love with other people's potential. You must meet them where they are."

Being willing to stand up for yourself and keeping positive people and influences around you are some of the most beneficial things you can do to achieve success in all areas of your life. As we stated earlier, being honest with yourself is also a key element to your success. If you find that you are being a negative or toxic person in someone else's world, this is a grand opportunity to look deep within yourself to seek the changes you may need to make. Communicate your newfound understandings through positive and loving words and actions toward those around you and see what kinds of amazing differences it can make. You might be pleasantly surprised.

Sometimes, we do things that can permanently damage relationships in our lives. In these instances, all we can do is take accountability for our actions or behaviors, apologize and take extreme ownership for them, do what we reasonably can to make it right, respect the wishes of others, and accept any consequences associated with our errors. It is important to note, in examples where relationships are damaged or even severed in their entirety, we must learn how to display compassion and forgiveness toward both ourselves and the other parties who may be involved. Understanding how to most effectively do this is an essential part of better loving ourselves, others, and will aid in ameliorating our overall self-healing processes.

Relationships are all about how we relate to others, and it is a part of our biological nature to seek out friends and people who we have commonalities with. You must understand that when you begin to make changes in your life, you may no longer have the same things in common anymore with those who you once related to. Do not be surprised if you begin to clash with certain individuals or if others in your life begin to drift away. On the contrary, do not be afraid to express your gratitude toward your family, friends, and the people you care for to show your love or appreciation to them in order to further strengthen your existing bonds.

A mentor of Nick's likes to repeat an anonymous quote, "You can change the people around you, or you can change the people around you." This means your goals could include cutting negative or toxic people out of your life, working to be a more positive influence to others, or making efforts to enhance the relationships with positive people who are already part of your life by setting definite times to visit and communicate with them more frequently.

If you are looking to meet new like-minded individuals, some ways could include attending networking meetings, social clubs, online groups, or other various social or educational events. You can also participate in group hobbies or activities, volunteer, get more involved with organizations that interest you, or you can seek friends, mentors, or coaches to better help guide you or make introductions to new individuals, activities, or events. Additionally, we encourage you to further read and educate yourself on strategies for how to best cultivate and maintain interpersonal relationships. The possibilities you can discover by getting yourself out there to meet and connect with new people are vast.

Now, you are going to want to consider all of the collective relationships in your life (family, friends, colleagues, teachers, therapists, coaches, etc.) and what aspects of them you feel you may want or need to change. In this section, do not focus on goals or relationships you may have with intimate or romantic partners. We will review these specific relationships in detail in the next chapter.

(Authors' Note: We have both gone through not only the hardships of cutting certain relationships from our lives but also through the challenging process of eliminating harmful traits from our own character. Taking these steps can be difficult, but they are some of the most empowering actions a person can take. They are part of our growth, healing, and maturity as human beings.

Sadly, some individuals face emotionally or physically abusive environments, whether from family members, close friends, or intimate partners. If you are in crisis, even if you happen to be under the age of eighteen, help is available through the National Domestic Violence Hotline at 1-800-799-7233. Other resources include www.Childhelp.org for children and teens, and www.TheHotline.org for information on relationship abuse and safety planning. While we hope you or those you care about will not ever need any of these resources, they do exist to support anyone going through these types of difficult situations).

So, how many new friends do you want to make? Who do you want to meet or visit? Who do you want to involve in your life more? Who do you feel you should involve in your life less?

(Authors' Note: If you do not wish to write in your copy of this book, or if you need a fresh template, please feel free to download this template separately by visiting www.TiltingTheBalance.com/Templates. If you need assistance on how to most effectively complete your template, visit the same hyperlink or you can revisit the detailed instructions in the "Personal Tasks" chapter).

You are now ready to complete your own "Family & Friend Relationships" template.

FAMILY & FRIEND RELATIONSHIPS

Item/Goal	Time Frame	Priority Level

Item/Goal	Time Frame	Priority Level

Today, in this category, I feel:

These factors or beliefs are holding me back in this category:

FAMILY & FRIEND RELATIONSHIPS

These are the boundaries and/or routines I need to implement and enforce:

Today, I am grateful for:

These are the most beneficial affirmations for me in this category:

CHAPTER 7
ROMANTIC RELATIONSHIPS

"The giving of love is an education in itself."
— Eleanor Roosevelt

Romantic relationships are an innate part of our biology. This is why most people tend to embrace their cultivation and seek to improve these types of relationships. When it comes to romantic relationships, the emphasis should again be on the principle of balance. Balanced romantic relationships tend to be more healthy ones.

Healthy romantic relationships are all about being balanced partners and counterparts to each other and ensuring that all parties feel free, safe, comfortable, supported, and loved. They also remain healthy when we maintain certain levels of individual independence and when we do not lose sight of our personal desires and dreams in the processes of developing these connections. This of course does not mean there cannot be areas in which we are dependent on our partners. It just means there must be sustained levels of overall balance within each relationship.

While the balance of independence and dependence is essential in all aspects of a relationship, there is no real set equation or formula for how exactly one is supposed to most effectively balance these forms of relationships. Each relationship is individualized and based on the separate needs of each individual partner. The variables for the success of the required balance in every relationship must be discussed and implemented by all of the parties who are romantically involved, and vary extravagantly based upon each individual's specific desires and needs. Each individual must also understand how to create and maintain their ideal balance of power within their relationships. In addition, they need to recognize the polarities and their roles associated with the masculine and feminine energies between themselves and their partners.

Basically, everybody is different in what they have to offer and in what things they want and expect from their partners. A healthy, balanced relationship dynamic means each partner is generally happy, within themselves as individuals and within the confines of the relationship, with most to all of their needs being met, whatever those needs may be. In this chapter, we want you to consider what it is you want in your dating or married life.

This is a good thing to consider regardless of whether you are single or already involved in an active relationship. Are you someone who is single and you are now ready to find a partner? Do you feel you need some form of change in your existing relationships? These considerations will help you figure out what it is you want in your romantic life, whether it is the desire to date multiple people, to get into a serious and committed relationship, or to improve or spice things up with an existing partner.

Where romantic relationships come with their associated challenges, they certainly have their benefits, too. Some of these benefits include living longer, healing quicker, feeling more connected and cutting down on loneliness, and not to mention... sex.

Yes, we said it! Having a healthy sex life has its own fringe benefits as well, such as an improved self-esteem, decreased stress and anxiety levels resulting in better sleep, the promotion of higher self-confidence, and the experience of other positive health-related benefits. Whether you are seeking a new romantic dating life, to further develop your current intimate relationships, or even wish to leave current partnerships, this is where you will begin to consider these goals. You also must be cognizant and aware of the consequences of not being safe with your well-being, with your emotions, and most especially with your sexual encounters. Failing to use caution, especially when meeting strangers, can lead to the detriment of your own personal physical safety, your mental well-being, and can cause you to contract sexually transmitted diseases and even have unplanned children. You must make safe and smart decisions, impose necessary boundaries, and not be afraid to trust and verify who people are, for the benefit of your own personal health and security.

You must also not be afraid to be your most authentic self or to be honest about your genuine desires. You need to be respectful of the other parties' desires, and should seek to ensure you are a strong and positive match with your prospective partners prior to jumping into commitments. We encourage you to throw any and all validation or approval-seeking behaviors out of the window, and to show up in such a way that your romantic partners feel comfortable doing the exact same. We recommend as well that you learn about your personal attachment style and the attachment styles of your romantic interests, as attachment styles impact the ways you form bonds with others and the manners in which they form their subsequent bonds with you.

We want to add that you should go into committed romantic relationships with the mindset to *give* — as a happy, healthy, confident, secure person. Too many people go into committed relationships seeking happiness from their partners and that is just not how it works. Author and relationships expert Coach Corey Wayne suggests that we must go into relationships happy, secure, and overflowing with love to share and give to our partners, and even potentially to the children that you may have together.

For long-term committed relationships, the goal is to find partnerships with those who will walk beside you and who will want to conquer the days together as your teammate.

This is why it is crucial to understand what unhealed traumas or insecurities you or your partners are bringing to the equation. The goal is to create healthy, interdependent relationships, and not those of a co-dependent nature.

The beginning of a romantic relationship is usually based on physical attraction. The strongest, long-lasting relationships are the ones created not out of the initial attraction we have in the first stages, but rather from the love we build and the trust and commitment we form, all through the effective communication we have, and from the collective experiences we share with our partners over the course of time.

You have to ask yourself, what is it that you want? More time with a significant other? To go on dates with new people or more dates with your current partner or partners? Are you uninterested in dating in general or for a set period of time? Do you want to get married? Where this could also fall under *"Family & Friend Relationships"* without having to be in a romantic involvement, do you want to grow your family by having or adopting children, or even pets? Do you want to end any existing romantic relationships or modify the parameters of any current involvements? If no, why not? If yes, why so? Do you want to learn more about in-depth relationship psychology such as attachment styles, argument styles, or intimacy techniques such as the art of Kama Sutra? Where are you in terms of your goals in creating or maintaining romantic relationships? Do you feel you could prosper from therapies, therapists, counselors, coaches, workshops, programs, books, retreats, or any resources that may provide educational, recreational, or other forms of positive benefits?

Some examples of goals could be to go on a certain number of dates per week with a potential new partner or with your current one, to meet a specific number of new potential partners every month, or to surprise your current significant other with something special.

(Authors' Note: We directly offer dating and relationship coaching for those seeking to cultivate new romantic involvements and also for those looking to improve their current, existing relationships. You can learn more or sign up for a coaching session today by visiting our website, www.TiltingTheBalance.com/LiveLearning. We also highly recommend quite a few books on dating and relationships. The first is Corey Wayne's How To Be A 3% Man. Although it is written more from a man's perspective, this book is great for members of any sex or sexual orientation as he explains detailed processes of how to effectively date and retain relationships in the masculine and feminine roles. Another great book on the polarity of feminine and masculine energy is The Way of the Superior Man by David Deida. Other great and apposite reads are The 5 Love Languages by Gary Chapman, an insightful read on how we prefer to give and receive love as individuals within romantic relationships and Men Are From Mars, Women Are From Venus by John Gray, an astounding book that teaches some of the fundamental differences in communication between men and women and feminine and masculine roles. We also recommend the book Attached: The New Science of Adult Attachment and How It Can Help You Find – and Keep – Love by Amir Levine, M.D., and Rachel S.F. Heller, M.A., a wonderful book that teaches about our biological attachment styles and how to recognize them in ourselves and our romantic partners. While these books primarily use heterosexual examples, the principles of polarity, attraction, and communication apply across all relationship types. You can adapt the concepts to fit your specific dynamic. To find all of these books available for purchase, visit www.TiltingTheBalance.com/OurFavoriteBooks).

(Authors' Note: If you do not wish to write in your copy of this book, or if you need a fresh template, please feel free to download this template separately by visiting www.TiltingTheBalance.com/Templates. If you need assistance on how to most effectively complete your template, visit the same hyperlink or you can revisit the detailed instructions in the "Personal Tasks" chapter).

You are now ready to complete your own "Romantic Relationships" template.

ROMANTIC RELATIONSHIPS		
Item/Goal	Time Frame	Priority Level

ROMANTIC RELATIONSHIPS

Item/Goal	Time Frame	Priority Level

Today, in this category, I feel:

These factors or beliefs are holding me back in this category:

ROMANTIC RELATIONSHIPS

These are the boundaries and/or routines I need to implement and enforce:

Today, I am grateful for:

These are the most beneficial affirmations for me in this category:

CHAPTER 8
SPIRITUALITY

"We are not human beings having a spiritual experience. We are spiritual beings having a human experience."
– Pierre Teilhard de Chardin

For so many of us around the world, spirituality is a core part of our existence and our self-meaning. The questions of life, where we come from, our philosophies of why and how to live, and our purpose for living are all pivotal questions about our realities.

Please understand that we are not here to force or push any kind of religion upon you. In fact, as co-authors, we both happen to have varying spiritual beliefs ourselves. We want you to consider your own spiritual beliefs and goals in this section. You may be Christian, Catholic, Jewish, Muslim, Hindu, Buddhist, Agnostic, Atheist, a Scientologist, or may identify with any other known religions out there. Your faith and beliefs may not even tie into any specific religion at all.

Religion is defined more as a specific set of organized beliefs and practices, whereas spirituality is more of an individual practice which has to do with self-peace and purpose. For example, meditation directly correlates with both spirituality and certain religious practices. Meditation fits the same and can also fall under other categories in this book, such as *"Hobbies, Passions, & Interests"* or within *"Physical Fitness & Mental Wellness."* You, of course, are free to have your own beliefs and set goals which specifically correspond with them. You may want to consider setting goals to perform certain activities such as meditation, yoga, prayer, visualizations, gratitude exercises, or affirmations in this category to help you reach whatever plains of spiritual enlightenment you may seek. Some of your goals may also include attending a religious or spiritual institution a specific amount of times per week or month, dedicating time to pray, reading scriptures, or learning about spiritual or religious history. They can even encompass making a dream board or using affirmations and gratitude practices to help manifest your dreams.

Manifestation also happens to be an interesting spiritual discussion in and of itself. The power of manifestation is the ability to harness the sight and feelings of achieving your desires in life through your visual imagination, thus prompting it to happen in your physical reality. People who strongly believe in the power of manifestation will tell you that everything they want in the universe is already theirs—the more clear, focused, and balanced your mind is, the faster and more precise your manifestations will be delivered into your reality. Much of this ties back to the philosophy of the *"Law of Attraction."*

There is also an abundance of other ways to practice spirituality and live spiritually. Astrology, horoscopes, numerology, herbology, using tarot cards, crystals, or essential oils, playing singing bowls, gongs, and other musical instruments, getting and giving massages, acupuncture, or cupping therapy, performing chakra exercises, and even taking certain kinds of drugs (which we of course do not either advise or condone you do illegally or irresponsibly)—all can be used as spiritual components of our lives. You may also notice how several of those activities can fall under some of the other *"10 Categories of Life"* as well.

Other goals can range from reading books or consuming educational content about spirituality, attending workshops or seminars, to following, enlisting, or hiring mentors or coaches who can aid you in learning and understanding more about your specific spiritual interests and can better guide you along your path toward spiritual enlightenment. So, in terms of your spiritual goals, write down whatever falls under your personal spirituality, the spiritual feats you want to accomplish, the practices you may want to perform, the plans you may want to make, and the actions you may need to take that will assist you in achieving your desired outcomes.

(Authors' Note: One of the ways we stay fulfilled in our spiritual lives is by periodically getting outside and immersed in nature. Another is by following both a morning and an evening routine which requires us to perform our specific spiritual practices. We also make plans every evening for the following day and ensure we hard schedule activities or practices that boost our levels of fulfillment in the spiritual areas of our lives when needed. In fact, we do this for a wide range of activities that fall under "The 10 Categories of Life."

There is tremendous power in following daily routines and pre-planning your days in order to best monitor and control your physical, mental, and spiritual health and well-being, as well as your overall levels of productivity).

(Authors' Note: If you do not wish to write in your copy of this book, or if you need a fresh template, please feel free to download this template separately by visiting www.TiltingTheBalance.com/Templates. If you need assistance for how to most effectively complete your template, visit the same hyperlink or you can revisit the detailed instructions in the "Personal Tasks" chapter).

You are now ready to complete your own "Spirituality" template.

SPIRITUALITY		
Item/Goal	Time Frame	Priority Level

Item/Goal	Time Frame	Priority Level

SPIRITUALITY

Today, in this category, I feel:

These factors or beliefs are holding me back in this category:

These are the boundaries and/or routines I need to implement and enforce:

Today, I am grateful for:

These are the most beneficial affirmations for me in this category:

CHAPTER 9
CHARITABLE GIVING

"It's not how much we give but how much love we put into giving."
— Mother Teresa

How many times in your life have you been in need of help and assistance? If you think about it, you have most likely received all sorts of care and nurturing to have even gotten to this point where you are able to read and comprehend the material in this book. Someone likely had to help teach you how to read. Before you were at an interval in your life where that was even possible, someone had to help feed you, provide you with food, clothing, shelter, and teach you the basic functions of daily living. You even needed help to be brought into the world, from the time of conception to the time of delivery.

Where some of us may receive far more care and nurture than others in our journeys, we all need help at times, and giving is an integral aspect of this world. Far too many people seem to miss this fact and are inclined to forget their roots.

Typically, people think about *"charity"* and *"giving"* solely as being financial or material actions. This is not always the case. Whether or not we may always have the financial assets or material resources available to help, there are various other ways by which we can aid and be charitable. One very important (and often overlooked) way is giving the gift of your time. As we examined earlier, our time is both limited and non-replaceable, making it our most invaluable asset. Some examples of giving your *time* for charity include volunteering for positive, progressive, and impactful organizations; mentoring others about how to understand a craft in which you are proficient; reading books to kids; playing music for people in nursing homes or hospitals; taking care of animals; the list continues. When we spend our time giving back, these activities tend to make us feel good, thus promoting positive thinking, and supporting a more positive, fulfilled life overall.

Famous author and motivational speaker Tony Robbins says, "The secret to living is giving." A primary reason his quote holds true is due to the reciprocity that is associated with giving. There have been research studies performed by numerous universities and neuroscientists all over the world that support the premise that our brains experience prolonged happiness after the act of giving, and there are beliefs that we are actually hardwired to serve others as human beings. This is why we often feel better when we give rather than when we receive; whether it be our time, money, knowledge, or other resources. There is truly great power in giving.

However, one thing to avoid at all costs is doing any type of charitable action for the sole purpose of boosting your ego through receiving attention, recognition, and popularity. This is often seen as self-serving, selfish, and disingenuous, which is why we encourage you to always have integrity and to be real and authentic in your charitable goals and actions. Quite frankly, you should abide by those principles in everything that you do. You should donate your time, money and/or knowledge to organizations or individuals that support causes you genuinely care about. At the end of the day, whatever it is you wish to give, it should always come from a sincere place of love and compassion.

The point we are alluding to again is to the pertinence of integrity. If you do not operate with integrity in all of your endeavors, you are less inclined to succeed and to experience more positive outcomes long-term. Being honest, authentic, having a strong moral compass, principles, and an honorable character will make you feel good about what you are doing and will build trust, respect, and appreciation with others you encounter. Your reputation is everything. As Benjamin Franklin so wisely stated, "It takes many good deeds to build a good reputation, and only one bad one to lose it."

Another approach to charitable giving is to partner with existing entities or to create your own organization (or multiple organizations even) that promote positive causes and provide resources in ways that are meaningful. Keep in mind that you may never understand how big of an impact you can have, create, or experience with the smallest of contributions. Sometimes, the smallest things in life are the ones that can have the most substantial, meaningful impacts.

(Authors' Note: Another great way to practice charitable giving in a small, yet significant way, is by setting the goal to perform one random act of kindness on a daily, weekly, or monthly basis. No matter how often you choose, even conducting a kind action only one time can have its range of positive associations. You can do something as simple as sending a loved one or friend a kind message, holding a door for someone, or returning a stranger's shopping cart. Other examples can include giving a small sum of money to a homeless person, or providing them with a meal or essential supplies. You could also volunteer a short amount of time to aid children, veterans, the elderly, or even animals. The possibilities of available actions are limitless when it comes to seeking to do something small, yet meaningful and significant for others).

Please understand this as well: In order to give, you need to have something to give. The reality is, each of us likely has *something* we can give. Some of us may have more time, money, knowledge, and resources to give than others where some will need to receive more blessings so that they, too, are capable of giving. We must not be afraid to ask for help where and when we need it, and we always need to do our best to find ways where we may be able to help based on our own individual circumstances.

We prompt you to ask yourself these questions: What causes do I genuinely care about and to which causes do I wish to donate my time, money, knowledge, resources, or energy? What kind of impact do I wish to create for those around me, for my community, for my environment, and for the very world I live in? What are the best ways I can provide assistance to others, to meaningful causes or for those in need, and how much aid can I actually provide? What philanthropic causes can I contribute to and how can I best support them? Could I benefit from additional educational content to relying upon mentors, coaches, or other guides to help me discover these answers? Once you have taken some time to carefully consider your options, begin writing down your *charitable goals*:

(Authors' Note: If you do not wish to write in your copy of this book, or if you need a fresh template, please feel free to download this template separately by visiting www.TiltingTheBalance.com/Templates. If you need assistance for how to most effectively complete your template, visit the same hyperlink or you can revisit the detailed instructions in the "Personal Tasks" chapter).

You are now ready to complete your own "Charitable Giving" template.

CHARITABLE GIVING		
Item/Goal	Time Frame	Priority Level

Item/Goal	Time Frame	Priority Level

Today, in this category, I feel:

These factors or beliefs are holding me back in this category:

These are the boundaries and/or routines I need to implement and enforce:

Today, I am grateful for:

These are the most beneficial affirmations for me in this category:

CHAPTER 10
FINANCIAL RESPONSIBILITIES

"Financial freedom is available to those who learn about it and work for it."
— Robert Kiyosaki

Financial responsibility is one of the most significant aspects to creating stability and independence in our lives. What is your ideal lifestyle and how do you envision it? Is it materialistic objects or assets you want, savings plans you desire, or a certain amount of annual or overall income you would like to attain? Exactly how much money would you need to accomplish your visions?

One thing we want to make very clear is the root principle that life is not all about money. You must understand this. We view money as a vessel that can help make you more of who you already are. There is a great quote from Manly P. Hall's classic book, *Ten Basic Rules for Better Living*: "In the course of years, the time will certainly come when we must ask ourselves how much we would be worth if we lost everything we had. The answer is obvious. Regardless of what we *have*, we are worth what we are."

When assessing your financial responsibilities, you should be looking at the income you would like to make, how much you want to save, how much you are willing to invest, and how much you are willing and able to give.

Perhaps one of the most viable aspects of maintaining financial stability is understanding exactly how much you will need to continuously earn so that you may accomplish your fiscal goals. Creating budgets and reviewing them periodically is a great step in the right direction because it allows you to follow a plan for your money, ensuring that you will have it appropriately allocated toward all of the required financial elements in your life. Sticking to a budget or set financial plan can also help you get out of current debts and can keep you from making poor financial decisions, which could lead to the accumulation of further non-performing debt. In numerous surveys performed across the United States, most people reported that budgeting helped them make better financial decisions and aided them to effectively forecast future financial plans. Tax, insurance, and estate planning, careful spending, and wise budgeting will all help you keep more of your hard-earned capital and generate future potential wealth.

(Authors' Note: We recommend the book I Will Teach You to Be Rich by Ramit Sethi. He delves deep into financial planning, budgeting, paying off debt, which credit cards to use, savings accounts to have, and much more. We also recommend reading Robert Kiosoki's Cash Flow Quadrant, to learn all about the difference between performing debt vs. non-performing debt. Another great book on basic savings and investment strategies is the classic, The Richest Man In Babylon by George S. Clason.

Find these books and more which we recommend about finance and investments on our website at www.TiltingTheBalance.com/OurFavoriteBooks).

Budgeting (and truthfully it is finances in general) is not always the most comfortable topic for everyone and sadly, most people tend to avoid their financial responsibilities as a result. Avoidance is far too common in instances when individuals are faced with dealing with non-performing debt or unpaid bills. Whatever your current financial situation, you must consider the entirety of your overall financial responsibilities.

Let us examine the landscape of most American households as an example. A study by GoBankingRates showed that sixty-six percent of Americans fear running out of money in retirement years, and an additional study by FINRA (Financial Industry Regulatory Authority) reported that only fifty-three percent have an emergency fund consisting of at least three months of savings. This shows that the way we think about money and budgeting is a fundamental issue in American society, and the importance of financial literacy is not only limited to Americans but also to the vast majority of individuals across the world.

As famous author John C. Maxwell says, "A budget is telling your money where to go instead of wondering where it went." However, financial budgeting is only one way of monitoring your spending and understanding your wherewithal to do so. The average American citizen spends over eighty percent of their income collectively on housing, transportation, insurance, and food alone. That does not leave much for buying other essentials, materials, gifts, paying for travel, or especially for making investments. This is why, in addition to being wise with your spending, we strongly advise that you learn what economic factors you may be affected by. We also urge you to educate yourself on how to most effectively manage your earnings, and encourage you to optimize them. This can be accomplished by figuring out strategies that can maximize your income, and can even include the creation of additional revenue streams.

To dive deeper, there are more factors to consider in terms of your income. Are there bills you can decrease or unnecessary expenses you can cut? Are there debts you can consolidate? What ways can you establish, build, fix, or utilize personal or business credit? Are there banking or lending relationships you can cultivate or any private capital resources you can utilize?

Do you want multiple revenue streams or just one stream of income? Do you want any income streams that are residual or passive? What is it that you desire financially? How much money do you want to make? Do you want an hourly wage or a higher hourly rate than one you may already have? Do you want a salary or an increase in your current salary? Do you want to have enough income saved to take a period of time off or take a mini-retirement where you do not have to work for months or even years?

This is also the place to consider your financial planning goals. Are there books, podcasts, or other educational resources you can turn to in order to improve your understanding of financial literacy and wealth management? Do you want to hire a financial advisor, a financial mentor, coach, or guide? Do you want to utilize new or review existing insurances, annuities, 401k's, IRA's, or other financial products? Do you need to hire an attorney to create a written will, complete estate planning, or create trusts or foundations? What are your specific financial planning needs?

As far as the questions go for how you want to make your money, we will review those in the next (and last) category of life, *"Business & Career Objectives."*

Think about your ideal lifestyle, what you desire financially, and how that can all help you, and even those you love and care about. Take your time to carefully consider your financial goals and responsibilities, and do not hold yourself back. **DREAM BIG!**

(Authors' Note: When it comes to your financial goals, the most important thing is not always whether you hit an exact number, but how much progress you make by aiming with intention. Setting bold targets can help you break free from limitations while creating a life with more options and opportunities. The reality is, money provides access to resources. It grants you the ability to invest further in your health, education, life experiences, material desires, and even in other people or causes you may care about.

To build a solid financial foundation, we encourage you to sharpen your professional skills, follow simple and consistent systems for managing money, and learn how to weigh highly calculated, high-reward risks against more secure and conservative choices. A key to financial freedom is enacting proven strategies that align with your values and long-term vision. We also recommend avoiding the trap of making all major financial decisions alone. Seek out mentors and professionals with a strong and proven history of helping others achieve real results. While you can absolutely pioneer creative income streams or investment strategies, we advise remaining cautious of leading solely with your ego.

Before rising to become a legendary investor and one of the wealthiest men alive, Ray Dalio learned this principle through costly mistakes rooted in overconfidence. Early in his career he made an incorrect market call that nearly wiped out his firm and forced him to let go of his entire team. That humbling setback inspired him to create what he calls idea meritocracy, a process where every fundamental decision is presented to a diverse circle for honest analysis and feedback.

In this open-style debate, titles and rankings do not matter, and only the strongest, most well-reasoned ideas prevail. Dalio's philosophy is clear: snap judgments create blind spots, whereas humility, varied input, and an unwavering commitment to truth yield smarter outcomes. Reality always trumps pride and ego.

Instead of committing to crucial decisions alone, seek out diverse perspectives and surround yourself with people who will challenge your ideas honestly, regardless of anyone's status or experience. The power of idea meritocracy extends beyond finance and can reshape how we communicate, make decisions, build relationships, and grow in all areas of life. You can explore this further in Ray Dalio's Principles: Life and Work, available at www.TiltingTheBalance.com/OurFavoriteBooks.

On the other side of financial pursuit, many people today remain stuck in survival mode. They are constantly working, worrying, and reacting, without realizing that financial clarity may be the very thing that sets them free. From Chuck Palahniuk's widely recognized novel, later adapted into the blockbuster film Fight Club, came the memorable line: "You are not your job. You are not how much money you have in the bank. You are not the car you drive. You are not the contents of your wallet."

There are countless individuals who appear financially successful, yet internally feel unhappy and unfulfilled. Often this happens because they pursued endeavors never aligned with their true purpose, believing that accumulated wealth would make them appear successful, provide validation or approval, or mask deeper insecurities. While money may offer a superficial sense of security or admiration, it rarely satisfies the deeper need for genuine, lasting self-worth.

True wealth is measured not in material possessions but in physical, mental, emotional, spiritual, and relational health. It is reflected in the legacy you leave, from the capacity of love you share and feel with both yourself and others, through the works you create, the quality and magnitude of those you empower, and the lasting impressions you make.

Ask yourself whether those you encounter feel seen, strengthened, or more aligned because of how you show up. Gauge your true wealth by the peace of mind you carry each day, understanding that money is merely a tool for generating options and impact rather than a metric of your personal identity. Let your focus remain not just on how you earn income, but on how you can contribute meaningfully to something greater than yourself.

No matter the financial reward, if what you do contradicts your integrity, the true cost may be your inner well-being. When you accept these principles, your financial life becomes a vehicle for empowered living. This shift leads to deeper connections, greater contributions, and lasting fulfillment aligned with your purpose. An additional read that powerfully reinforces this message is Robin Sharma's The Wealth Money Can't Buy: The 8 Hidden Habits to Live Your Richest Life, which you can also find at www.TiltingTheBalance.com/OurFavoriteBooks).

(Authors' Note: If you do not wish to write in your copy of this book, or if you need a fresh template, please feel free to download this template separately by visiting www.TiltingTheBalance.com/Templates. If you need assistance on how to most effectively complete your template, visit the same hyperlink or you can revisit the detailed instructions in the "Personal Tasks" chapter).

You are now ready to complete your own "Financial Responsibilities" template.

FINANCIAL RESPONSIBILITIES

Item/Goal	Time Frame	Priority Level

Item/Goal	Time Frame	Priority Level

Today, in this category, I feel:

These factors or beliefs are holding me back in this category:

These are the boundaries and/or routines I need to implement and enforce:

Today, I am grateful for:

These are the most beneficial affirmations for me in this category:

CHAPTER 11
BUSINESS & CAREER OBJECTIVES

"Nothing will work unless you do."
— Maya Angelou

This is the final area in *"The 10 Categories of Life."* We are now that much closer to putting all of your goals and desires into fully thought-out, planned, actionable steps. As it relates to your business or career, do you work a conventional "nine-to-five" job? Are you an independent contractor, coach, or consultant? Do you own your own business, own multiple businesses, or are you in the process of building a new business enterprise altogether? Do you enjoy what you do? Do you enjoy your customers? Do you enjoy your colleagues, vendors, supervisors, or business partners? Are you passionate about your current business roles? If not, is the work you are performing serving as a positive benefit to you or is it projecting you to a position where you want to be from a more long-term, futuristic goals perspective?

Are you a high school graduate looking to attend college or to immediately focus on an entrepreneurial journey? Maybe you are an older adult who wishes to embark on that very same endeavor, or you want to go back and become a college student again to obtain certain degrees, certifications, or licenses. What if you are an athlete aspiring to compete collegiately, professionally, or even dream of participating or representing your country in the Olympics? Do you want to win a Super Bowl, the Stanley Cup, the World Series, the Heisman, a Grammy, an Oscar, or any other significant award? Are you striving to coach athletes on a business or professional level?

Whatever your dreams may be, with the online education space and social media both experiencing a massive increase in total growth, there are now more ways than ever to learn in the world and gain positive exposure for yourself, especially on the internet! As far as learning goes, you can take unaccredited courses and gain access to the information you may be seeking from highly educated, uncredentialed professionals.

There is, of course, an abundance of avenues where you can find accredited courses for degrees, certifications, and licenses, along with a plethora of credentialed coaches, consultants, and mentors available to learn from as well. There are books, articles, magazines and other content you can read or listen to along with seminars, workshops, and individual classes you can attend. In the event online learning is not for you, you can also use the internet to locate where you can find all of these resources offline and in person.

As it relates to gaining exposure for yourself, you can use the internet to promote content or videos sharing information or performing activities that can get you recognized and/or add credibility to your endeavors. You can also use social media platforms and other online platforms to forge new, meaningful connections that can help project you forward professionally. Out of all of the times in life we could have existed, these are the resources we have at our disposal today, and it is wildly fascinating! We are currently only in the beginning of an era with how our lives are becoming increasingly more intermingled and intertwined online. This also gives us all a tremendous opportunity that has never existed before! The present window to earn a meaningful income and gain relevant exposure online is one-hundred-percent real and viable, and there is a huge wave of options and opportunities at this time in our history.

(Authors' Note: The world of business and education is our passion. We offer workshops, seminars, and direct coaching for entrepreneurs who are looking to launch their own businesses, who want to grow or refine their existing ones, and for those who want to learn how to take their operations online. For more details, please visit our website, www.TiltingTheBalance.com/LiveLearning).

So, what do you want? Is it a new job or career? A new promotion within your current company? Do you want to start your own small business? Do you want to grow or scale your small business into a larger operation or even into a megacorporation? Do you want to invest in a business, buy into a franchise, or purchase an existing business? Do you want to stay in the same industry you currently work in or do you wish to venture into a new one? Do you want to join a new team or better utilize coaches or other professional connections to attain your desired outcomes? Is there something you dream of doing but need further education in order to be empowered to do so?

Are you willing to go back to school or to enlist in educational programs so that you can acquire the required degrees, certificates, licenses, or credentials that you need? Do you have your Associate's Degree and want your Bachelor's? Do you want your Master's or are you looking to get a Doctorate? Do you want to graduate from school as Valedictorian or with honors such as Summa Cum Laude? Do you want certain credentials at the end of your name in your current industry or for one you are seeking to join? Are you willing and ready to sign up for the classes and courses you need to take or for the workshops or seminars that will teach you what you need to know?

Another meaningful factor to take into consideration is what your dream would look like if money were no issue at all. The facet of finance stops a lot of individuals in their tracks when it comes to taking the appropriate steps to learn about or to invest in their own businesses. This is a good place to weigh out your financial responsibilities against your business initiatives.

Another great idea you can contemplate is the possibility of turning one of your hobbies, passions, or interests into a sustainable business model. For example, if your current hobby, passion, or interest is to take photos, can you take that dream and convert it into a real, revenue-generating photography business? Oftentimes, we can refocus our hobbies, passions, and interests into something that makes us legitimate money. Sometimes it can be a little more rewarding participating in our hobbies while we are simultaneously benefiting from them financially. On the contrary, sometimes converting our passions into work can diminish the love or enjoyment we may have for that very passion. This is something to consider when you are assessing both your business and financial goals.

(Authors' Note: Our business coaching services specialize in training you on the fundamental skills of building, growing, and scaling your business. We can aid with business plans, fundraising, marketing, sales strategies, and much more. Learn more and sign up today by visiting www.TiltingTheBalance.com/LiveLearning).

Another aspect of setting your business goals is contemplating what business skills or resources you may need in order to be successful in your endeavors and operations. Do you need to finish or learn how to complete a business plan? Do you need to acquire new skills or apply ones you already know? Do you need to learn fundraising, sales, marketing, networking, leadership, or other essential skills? Do you need to build, learn more about, or implement fundraising, sales, marketing, or networking campaigns? Do you need to hire other companies or individuals to perform these or other required business services for you? Do you need to hire, fire, or train employees or vendors? Do you want to outsource or delegate functions of your professional duties and responsibilities, better organize your operations, or even utilize artificial intelligence resources? What software programs are available that might aid you in your business goals and operations? What professional associations, networks, or strategic partnerships can help you advance or grow?

One of the most paramount questions you can ask yourself is what elements of your life may be holding you back from taking the business steps you know you want or need to take? This is also a question you should ask yourself for all of the areas of your life. The answer to this question may lie deep in the other *"10 Categories of Life"* and it is beneficial to take the time to explore whether or not you may be making poor choices and decisions with how you spend your time and even with whom you spend your time that may be negatively affecting you.

As you think about all of your business goals, we also urge you to remain genuine. Not only to yourself but to others as well. Oftentimes, the most successful businesses solve the most significant problems for others. People often start working jobs or create new businesses solely for the money and nothing else. We implore you not to fall into this trap. When we set out to do the right thing and chase our ideas apart from just the money, the money will usually come. Make sure that you follow the principles that we provided herein and truly believe in whatever product or service you are offering, because this will greatly add value to your efforts, your mission, your customers, your company, and your overall success and well-being.

(Authors' Note: This is also another great time for the reminder to always operate with integrity. As we stated, if you do not operate with integrity in all of your endeavors, you are more inclined to not gain the results you desire and to experience more negative outcomes long-term; especially in the realm of business).

There is an array of questions you can ask yourself in this space. For most of us with aspirations, our dreams are one-hundred-percent possible. However, most of us do not take the chances or the action steps needed. Most often, it is out of fear. We fear rejection, we fear failure, and sometimes we even fear success itself. The best thing you can do is make the time to think as in-depth about your business desires, dreams, and needs as possible.

Without reaching for our dreams, how can we ever obtain them? How would we ever know what we truly could or could not make happen without making the attempt?

(Authors' Note: If you do not wish to write in your copy of this book, or if you need a fresh template, please feel free to download this template separately by visiting www.TiltingTheBalance.com/Templates. If you need assistance for how to most effectively complete your template, visit the same hyperlink or you can revisit the detailed instructions in the "Personal Tasks" chapter).

You are now ready to complete your own "Business & Career Objectives" template.

BUSINESS & CAREER OBJECTIVES

Item/Goal	Time Frame	Priority Level

Item/Goal	Time Frame	Priority Level

Today, in this category, I feel:

These factors or beliefs are holding me back in this category:

These are the boundaries and/or routines I need to implement and enforce:

Today, I am grateful for:

These are the most beneficial affirmations for me in this category:

CHAPTER 12

Assessing Your Current Life Balance: The 10 Categories Exercise

"Balance is not something you find, it's something you create."
— Jana Kingsford

Congratulations! You have reached an exciting milestone where it is time to build on the progress you have made and begin taking real action toward achieving the success you want. This is where your journey truly becomes both rewarding and transformative. Now that you have a clear understanding of *The 10 Categories of Life* and a deeper awareness of your own mindsets, it is time to turn these concepts into actionable steps. As we have explored, dreams and desires become far more achievable when they are structured as goals.

To support you, we have crafted a simple yet powerful exercise to assess where you currently stand in each category of life. This exercise will highlight areas where you are thriving and reveal where your greatest focus and attention are needed. By identifying these key areas, you will gain clarity to take intentional steps and begin "tilting the balance" toward the life you desire.

This exercise is not about perfection, but about gaining further progress and self-awareness. It serves as a compass, guiding you toward the goals that matter most. By the end of this chapter, you will have a clearer understanding of where to focus your energy and which goals will create the greatest impact.

In the next chapter, we will dive deeper into crafting *S.M.A.R.T. Goals* to turn your aspirations into actionable, achievable outcomes. For now, let us focus on identifying your starting points so you can confidently take the first steps toward meaningful change and lasting results.

How to Complete this Exercise and Visualize Your Current Life Balance:

Step 1: Read through each category description below. Take a moment to reflect on what each area represents and how it aligns with your life right now.

Step 2: Rate each category on a scale from 0 to 10. A score of 0 indicates an area needing significant attention, while a score of 10 reflects complete fulfillment, success, and alignment in that part of your life.

Step 3: Using the pie chart provided below, shade each section based on your rating. The pie chart is divided into 10 segments, each corresponding to a category, with markers for each number from 0 to 10. For example, if you rate *"Physical Fitness & Mental Wellness"* as a 5, shade up to the midpoint of that section. We suggest lightly shading with a pencil so you can erase and reuse this chart in your book or download a fresh copy anytime from www.TiltingTheBalance.com/Templates.

Step 4: Reflect on your results. The completed chart provides a visual representation of your current life balance and circumstances. The unshaded sections will reveal which areas may need more attention, while the fuller sections will show where you are currently thriving and experiencing success.

As you review your chart, take a moment to consider how making improvements in one area could inherently elevate others. For instance:
- Improving your business could lead to increased financial resources, enabling you to fund more meaningful experiences, invest in self-care, or spend greater time with loved ones.
- Enhancing your physical health might boost your energy and confidence, helping you become more productive in your career or more present in your personal life.
- Strengthening your relationships with family or friends could provide emotional stability and motivation, positively impacting other aspects of your life.

To help you visualize what this completed exercise would look like, here is a small example of a completed pie chart:

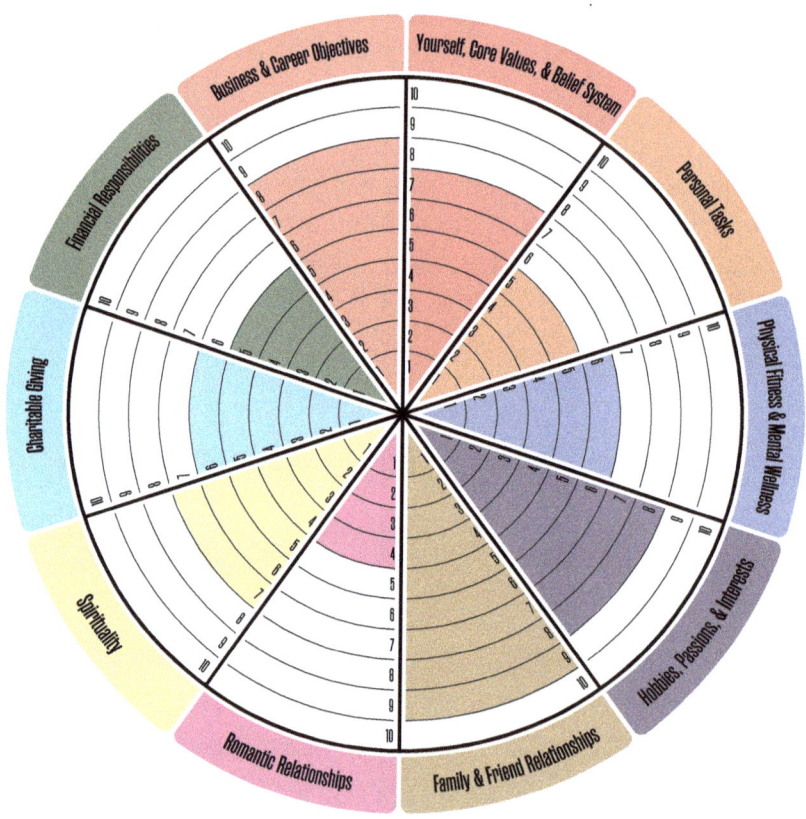

This exercise is not just about identifying what areas within *"The 10 Categories of Life"* need improvement, but also about seeing how the different aspects of your life are interconnected. By focusing on one specific area, you may find that growth naturally spills over into others, creating a domino effect of greater progress and fulfillment.

1. The Self, Core Values, & Belief Systems

Take a moment to reflect on how well you truly know yourself. Do you feel a deep sense of self-awareness and understanding? Are you holding yourself to high standards and living in true alignment with your values? Consider how you view yourself, both in your character and actions. Do you feel inner peace, gratitude, and confidence about who you are?

Think about your perspective on the world and your place within it. Do you view life through a lens of possibility, or does negativity cloud your mindset? Do you see yourself as someone who brings joy and positivity to others, or do you find yourself feeling rather disconnected or critical? This category examines how well your values, character, and mindset align with your current life path.

Rate this area on your graph, with 0 representing misalignment or total dissatisfaction and 10 representing complete alignment, fulfillment, and a positive outlook.

2. Personal Tasks

Take a moment to reflect on how efficiently and effectively you manage your personal and operational tasks. Do you feel organized and in control, or are these tasks a constant source of stress or overwhelm? Are you proactive in staying on top of your responsibilities, or do they often pile up or feel like a burden?

Consider how you handle everyday tasks like errands, chores, and general organization. Do you regularly complete things like laundry, dishes, grocery shopping, paperwork, etc., or do they linger on your to-do list and create a sense of disorder? Rate this area on your graph, with 0 representing complete chaos and disarray and 10 representing total organization, efficiency, and mastery of daily tasks.

3. Physical Fitness & Mental Wellness

Take a moment to reflect on your physical fitness and mental wellness. How active and fit do you feel in your daily life? Are you prioritizing your overall well-being by engaging in regular exercise and maintaining healthy habits? In addition to how you feel physically, how do you feel mentally? Do you feel balanced, resilient, and in control of your emotional health? Are you seeking the proper support to work through challenges and maintain mental well-being?

Consider your commitment to self-care practices. Do you consistently make time for proper nutrition, adequate rest, and stress management? Are you engaging in activities that support both your physical vitality and emotional stability?

Rate this area on your graph, with 0 representing complete neglect of your health and wellness and 10 representing optimal physical fitness and mental harmony.

4. Hobbies, Passions, & Interests

Take a moment to reflect on the hobbies, passions, and interests that bring joy and creativity into your life. Are you investing time in activities that lift you up and provide a sense of fun or fulfillment? Are you regularly engaging in things you love to do simply for the joy they bring, or have these initiatives taken a backseat to other responsibilities?

Consider the ways you spend your time outside of work or other obligations. Are you exploring creative outlets like painting, reading, or music? Do you find enjoyment in physical activities such as sports or gardening, or are you learning new skills that excite and inspire you?

Rate this area on your graph, with 0 representing complete absence of personal interests and enjoyment and 10 representing rich engagement in fulfilling activities and passionate pursuits.

5. Family & Friend Relationships

Take a moment to reflect on your relationships with family and friends. Are you nurturing these connections and dedicating quality time to the people who matter most? Do you feel a sense of closeness, support, and mutual care within these relationships? Are there connections that need strengthening or others that may no longer serve your growth?

Consider how you maintain these bonds. Are you making time for regular phone calls, celebrating special occasions, or gathering for family dinners? Are you showing up for social events and being present during times of need?

Rate this area on your graph, with 0 representing disconnection and strain in key relationships and 10 representing deep, nurturing bonds with those who matter most.

6. Romantic Relationships

Take a moment to reflect on the quality and fulfillment of your romantic life. Consider how connected, appreciated, and loved you feel in your romantic endeavors. Are you experiencing a sense of closeness and mutual understanding, or is there room for growth in how you approach and experience romantic connections?

Think about what makes romantic relationships fulfilling for you. Are you experiencing the level of intimacy, communication, and shared experiences that align with your values? Are you nurturing meaningful connections that bring joy and satisfaction to your life?

Rate this area on your graph, with 0 representing complete dissatisfaction with your romantic life and 10 representing deep fulfillment in your romantic connections.

7. Spirituality

Take a moment to reflect on your sense of connection to something greater than yourself. How deeply do you feel connected to a source of meaning, purpose, or inner peace? Spirituality can take many forms, from religious practices to moments of quiet reflection, meditation, or simply finding solace in nature.

Consider the ways you nurture this connection in your life. Are you regularly engaging in practices like meditation, prayer, yoga, religious study, or acts of gratitude? Do you find time to reflect, seek guidance, or connect with the natural world to cultivate a sense of calm and meaning? This category is about assessing how fulfilled you feel in your spiritual life and the role it plays in bringing peace and purpose to your life.

Once you have reflected, rate this area on your graph, with 0 representing a complete lack of spiritual connection, fulfillment, or practices and 10 representing a deep, meaningful sense of spiritual connection, inner peace, and consistent engagement in spiritually nourishing activities.

8. Charitable Giving

Take a moment to reflect on your contributions to others and the world around you. How often do you give back, support causes you care about, or offer help to those in need? Do you feel that you are making a meaningful impact, or is this an area where you could invest more time and energy?

Consider the ways you contribute. Are you volunteering your time, donating to causes that align with your values, or providing resources like money, skills, or emotional support to those who need it? Reflect on how your actions align with your desire to make a positive difference in the lives of others. This category is about assessing the extent to which you are giving back and contributing to others or causes beyond yourself.

Once you have reflected, rate this area on your graph, with 0 representing no charitable giving, volunteering, or community involvement and 10 representing consistent, meaningful, and impactful efforts to support others, give back, and make a positive difference in the world.

9. Financial Responsibilities

Take a moment to reflect on your financial responsibilities and how they impact your overall peace of mind. Are you managing your finances effectively and feeling secure in your ability to meet your needs? Do you feel confident about your financial decisions, or is this an area that causes stress or uncertainty?

Think about the key aspects of your financial health. Are you creating and following a budget, saving for the future, or working to pay off debts? Are you investing wisely or planning for long-term financial goals? Reflect on how your financial habits and choices support your current and future stability. This category is about assessing your sense of financial security and how effectively you manage your responsibilities in this area.

Once you have reflected, rate this area on your graph, with 0 representing severe financial instability, poor money management, and overwhelming financial stress and 10 representing optimal financial health, security, and confidence in your ability to meet your needs and achieve your financial goals.

10. Business & Career Objectives

Take a moment to reflect on your career or business pursuits to identify how fulfilled you feel in this area of your life. Are you progressing toward your professional goals and finding purpose in the work you do? Do you feel a sense of accomplishment and satisfaction, or is there room for greater growth, alignment, or motivation?

Think about the key elements of your professional life. Are you meeting important career milestones, pursuing meaningful business ventures, or achieving a healthy sense of balance? Consider how your current role or efforts align with your long-term vision and aspirations. This category is about evaluating your sense of purpose, progress, and fulfillment in your career or business.

Once you have reflected, rate this area on your graph, with 0 representing complete dissatisfaction, lack of progress, or misalignment with your professional goals and 10 representing optimal fulfillment, achievement, and a deep sense of purpose and satisfaction in your work.

Putting It All Together

Take your time to ensure you have accurately filled out your pie chart and rated each category. Once completed, take a deep look at your results. What stands out? Which areas are thriving, and which need more attention? This exercise is your starting point for everything else that follows in this book.

Keep in mind that it is normal to have varying levels of satisfaction across different areas of life. A perfect balance with 10s in every category is neither realistic nor necessary for overall happiness. Instead, aim for scores of 7 or higher, as these reflect a strong sense of fulfillment and alignment.

Any scores of 6 or below indicate opportunities for growth. If you do find some lower scores, do not be discouraged. This is where your efforts can have the greatest impacts. As you complete this exercise, remember that it is a foundational tool for understanding your priorities and directing your energy toward meaningful change.

To enhance your reflection, we want you to ask yourself two simple but powerful questions. The first is, what changes, such as actions, habits, mindsets, or behaviors, can you focus on that would raise your scores across any categories in need of improvement?

The next is, which single area, if improved, would naturally cause your scores and fulfillment in other categories to rise as well, without needing to focus on them directly? These answers will provide valuable insight into what areas of your life may need the most attention right now.

This clarity will guide you in setting effective "S.M.A.R.T. Goals," which we will cover in the next chapter, and will also prepare you for the life-changing "3-4-30 Challenge℠" discussed in the chapter immediately after.

Since life and your priorities are always evolving, revisiting this exercise regularly will help you stay aligned with your goals and maintain momentum. Use it whenever you need direction or feel off balance, and especially before setting your "S.M.A.R.T. Goals" or embarking on a new "3-4-30 Challenge℠." By checking in with this assessment periodically, you can recalibrate your efforts to ensure they remain intentional and impactful.

As you continue, remember to embrace the insights you have gained and the actions ahead. Each step brings you closer to the life you envision, with greater balance and fulfillment in every category of life.

(Authors' Note: If you do not wish to write in your copy of this book, or if you need a fresh template, please feel free to download this template separately by visiting www.TiltingTheBalance.com/Templates).

You are now ready to complete your own "Assessing Your Current Life Balance: The 10 Categories Exercise" template.

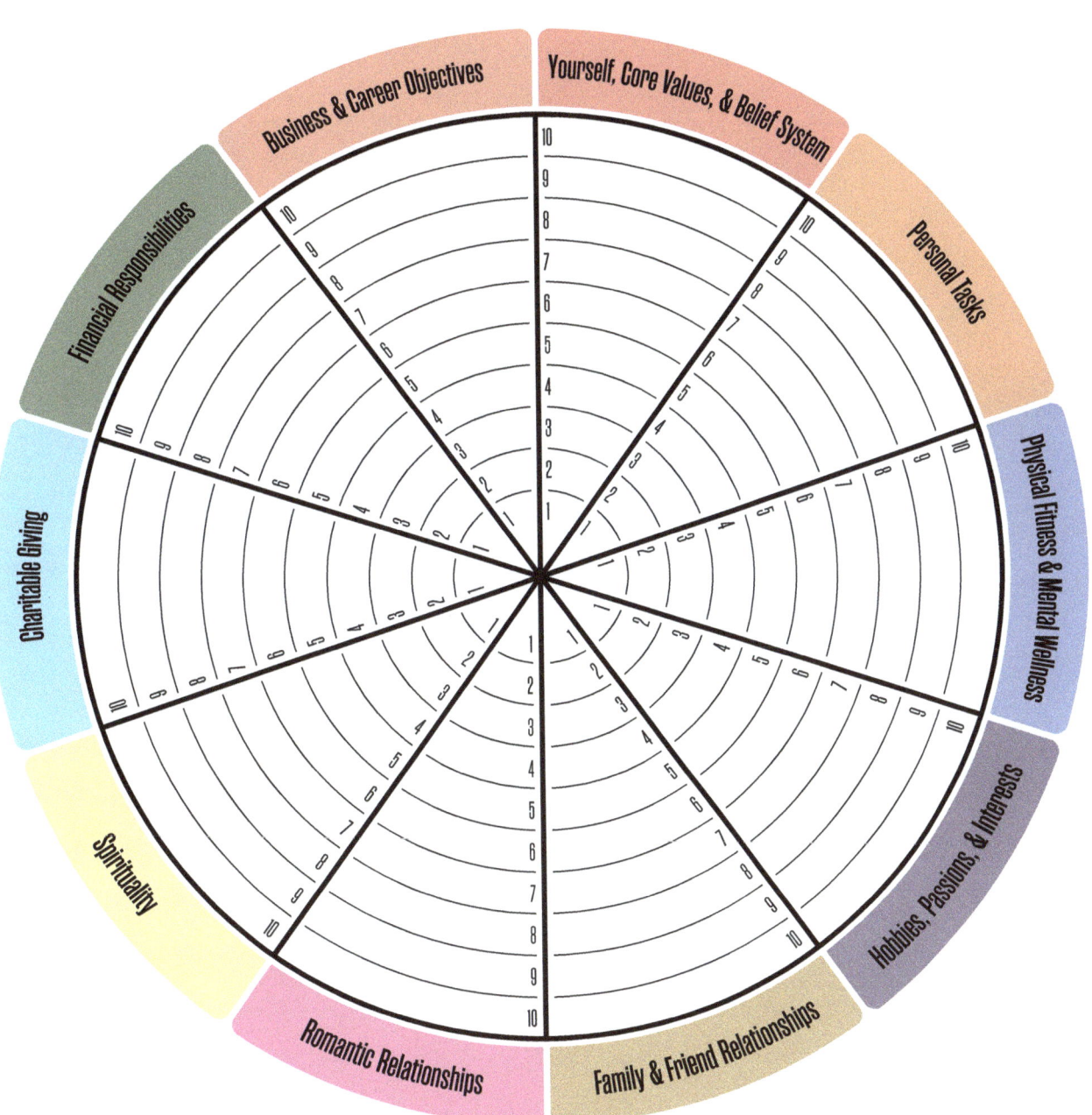

CHAPTER 13
LET'S GET "S.M.A.R.T."

"When it is obvious that the goals cannot be reached,
don't adjust the goals, adjust the action steps."
— Confucius

Now that you have read, understood, and completed all of your templates for each of *"The 10 Categories of Life,"* how does it feel? Do you feel empowered? Motivated? Relieved? Excited? Do you maybe even feel a bit overwhelmed?

This section is designed to help you stay on a positive trajectory by formatting your goals and desires into a real, viable, and executable plan of actionable steps.

In the 1981 article, "There's a S.M.A.R.T. way to write management goals and objectives" developed by George Doran, Arthur Miller, and James Cunningham, the concept of *"S.M.A.R.T. Goals"* was first introduced.

We are advocates for using the *"S.M.A.R.T. Goals"* methodology as a guide in your processes of goal-setting. The basis of *"S.M.A.R.T. Goals"* is that your goals must meet the following criteria: the goals must be specific, measurable, attainable, realistic, and have a timeline, hence the acronym: *"S.M.A.R.T."*

We also believe that to be in a position where you can achieve the results you desire and dream, you must comprehend that there are three major components to understand about each of your desired outcomes. The first component is to consider exactly what results you **desire**. Take a moment to ask yourself exactly what all it is that you wish to accomplish. We recommend that you revisit and use the prior templates that you completed throughout *"The 10 Categories of Life"* to help you begin to set some of your desires into real, tangible *"S.M.A.R.T. Goals."*

The second component is to consider your **drive** to achieve these desired results and to question exactly why you are motivated to attain each specific outcome. The point is to ponder why you want to achieve each specific goal and why the outcome of achieving each goal is so desirable to you. We strongly encourage you to question why you find each goal to be so desirable until you are left with the understanding of the root for each specific desire. This methodology will directly aid in setting and prioritizing your goals. You may even find that by thinking through all of your prospective goals this way, some of them may fall off altogether.

The third and final constituent is to begin questioning exactly what actionable steps you must take to obtain each specific **outcome** for the goals you are seeking to accomplish.

The bottom line is if you do not have enough of an understanding as to why you desire to accomplish your goals, you will most likely lack the drive (or motivation) needed to take the necessary actionable steps to accomplish them and earn the outcomes you want. You will also most likely not gain the understanding for exactly what steps you may need to take so that you can achieve them.

This is why using the method of setting *"S.M.A.R.T. Goals"* once you identify your desire, drive, and outcome for each specific goal can be so powerful in helping you to succeed.

To help provide further clarity on how to properly utilize these strategies, we are going to use the example of having the desire to lose weight as being set and structured as a *"S.M.A.R.T. Goal."*

To begin, we must of course first question the desire, the drive, and the projected outcome.

Example:

Desire: To lose weight.

Drive: To be healthier and have more energy, to be sick less often, to look and feel better, to live longer, and to reap all of the benefits of healthy living.

Outcome: To lose fifteen pounds in ninety days by creating and implementing both a diet and workout regimen.

Now that we have identified the desire, the drive for why we want it, and what outcome we are anticipating, we can begin formatting our goals using the *"S.M.A.R.T. Goals"* formula.

When implementing the *"S.M.A.R.T. Goals"* method, the first step is to ensure your goals are **specific**. Your goals need to be specific enough to where there is an easily identifiable result that comes with the accomplishment of each goal. Using our example of having the desire to lose weight is a specific result, right?

The second step is to ensure your goals are **measurable** so you can create clear and identifiable criteria to indicate exactly when your goals have been accomplished. In our example of wanting to lose weight, let us use the measurable example that the goal is to lose fifteen pounds. This is a measurable result.

As the third step in the process, you must be certain that your goals are indeed **achievable**. Continuing with our example, if the goal is to lose fifteen pounds, you must ask yourself whether or not that is in fact a truly achievable goal for you. We understand this example may not apply to everyone, as not everyone has fifteen pounds to lose while still remaining healthy or that not everyone is capable of doing or achieving certain things due to possible mental or physical limitations. This is a substantial point. Your goals must be achievable and you must draw the understanding of whether or not you truly believe that they are in fact one-hundred-percent possible for you to accomplish.

The real magic is in your belief that the goals you set can come to fruition and actualize in your reality.

The fourth step in the *"S.M.A.R.T. Goals"* process is to be sure that your goals are **realistic.** Your goals must be both physically and mentally realistic and you must be adequately prepared and committed to accomplishing them. Again, referencing our example, if the goal is to lose fifteen pounds, even if it may be achievable, you must consider whether or not it is realistic to take upon that challenge based on your own present circumstances at the time of setting and striving toward your goal.

The fifth and final step in the *"S.M.A.R.T. Goals"* process is to ensure that you have an anchored **time frame** associated with your goals. We believe you should have a specific, realistic, measurable, and even motivating time frame associated with accomplishing each of your goals. Say that, using our weight loss example again, the goal is to lose fifteen pounds in ninety days. For most, ninety days is a pretty specific, measurable, achievable, realistic, and motivating time frame needed to accomplish that goal. What about sixty days though? Is that enough time or would that likely be applying too much pressure? This is where you need to consider the repercussions of your set time frames. The example provided prompts the question as to whether or not it is even healthy for someone to lose that much weight in such a short time period, or whether or not that amount of weight loss is even physically possible for each and every individual.

The time frame of your goals needs to be realistic based on your personal schedule, your own physical and mental limitations, and must be factored in with all of your other potential goals and responsibilities. You must be sure that the time frames you set are not too long or too short, that they will not cause too much unnecessary pressure, and that they will not have pernicious effects on other initiatives which are also priorities to you. When applying *"S.M.A.R.T. Goals"* to your desires, the trick is to not associate rigorous or unrealistic time frames that could be detrimental to your drive, motivation, relationships, overall initiatives, and even your physical and mental health. It is important to set time frames which will push you in a more balanced way toward accomplishing the goal. Life is more of a marathon, not a sprint. You must understand how to balance all of your energy so that you can remain positive and keep taking consistent action.

In summary, each and every one of us has different desires. We all have individual circumstances in our lives along with our own personal limitations and current available resources. Consequently, these factors may or may not aid or hinder the accomplishment of certain results and desired outcomes in your life. You must take these factors into consideration when contemplating your goals. The reality is, the more goals you have, the more time it is most likely going to take for you to accomplish all of them collectively.

(Authors' Note: As we stated prior, remember that it is acceptable (and inevitable) to fall short of achieving your goals in your allotted time frames. There can be situations and circumstances which may arise that are outside of your control, or sometimes there may be aspects associated that you are accountable for in failing to meet your set deadlines. Regardless, understand that you are only human and not perfect. Your processes of taking action in general are pushing you further ahead toward accomplishing your overall goals and dreams more so than where you were when you initially got started).

The more pressure you put on yourself, the more you will either push yourself to accomplish your goals faster, or the more you will push yourself to have to stop and/or try again. All of the variables we have urged you to consider throughout this chapter are most likely different for everyone. This is also a huge reason why we recommend using *"The 3-4-30 Challenge[SM]"* as a way to help yourself in getting started so that you will not allow yourself to become intimidated or inundated by large goals and lengthy timelines which may help push or lead you away from the results you desire. We want you to build the momentum toward the belief that you can accomplish your goals, to increase your confidence levels, remain balanced and healthy, and know that you are capable of doing anything you put your mind to.

We have assembled a template that will aid you in setting your "S.M.A.R.T. Goals." First, using the "S.M.A.R.T. Goals" formula we have reviewed with your goals being specific, measurable, achievable, and realistic, you will want to input each specific goal you may have under the Item / Goal section in the second column. We encourage you to go back through all of the templates you have completed previously throughout this book so you can formulate those ideas into "S.M.A.R.T. Goals."

The third column labeled Set Date is where you will enter the initial date you set your goal, and the fourth column labeled By Date is where you will input the last component of the "S.M.A.R.T. Goals" formula with the associated time frame for each goal.

You can always come back and reuse this template beginning your goals on any particular date. Here are some examples:

	S.M.A.R.T. GOALS		
Done	Item/Goal	Set Date	By Date
☐	Lose fifteen pounds in ninety days.	(03/01/YY)	(05/29/YY)
☐	Write and publish a book in six months.	(03/01/YY)	(09/01/YY)
☐	Write chapters 3-5 of the book in the next thirty days.	(04/17/YY)	(05/16/YY)
☐	Create a budget this week and list all my expenses.	(05/08/YY)	(05/13/YY)
☐	Complete X assignment/tasks today	(06/19/YY)	(06/19/YY)

We could provide hundreds of thousands (or more) examples, but the point is that you can use this template to set daily goals, goals that are further out in the future, and can utilize it any time to help set, prioritize, and achieve any of your goals.

The next component of the template is the first column on the left side labeled Done. Once you complete a goal, you will want to check the box or fill it in to mark your goal complete. There is innate power to this, as checking or marking the boxes can give you a small hit of dopamine and can encourage you to continue to achieve your goals so that you may experience the feeling of checking them off as you complete them while reaping the benefits of physically seeing your goals being accomplished. It also gives you something to look back and reflect on as you continue forward along in your endeavors.

Adversely, when you do not achieve your goals, seeing boxes unchecked and feeling the experience of having not accomplished your goals can sometimes be challenging. This process can increase your self-awareness, improve your accountability, and can subsequently end up being rather enlightening and sometimes even motivating as a result.

What we strongly encourage is for you to be brutally honest with yourself when you do not achieve your goals and to use the lack of achieving your desired outcomes as learning opportunities. This is where the *Notes* section at the end of the template comes into effect. Anytime you do not complete a goal or get to check or mark a box, we want you to write in the Notes section a brief explanation as to exactly why you were unable to accomplish that individual goal. You can give explanations such as: procrastination, prioritized other things, failed to remember, sickness and/or injury, special circumstances, or simply a change of heart, etc. You can use quick notes like the examples we just provided or, feel free to write longer, more detailed explanations.

The Notes section is designed to serve as a self-awareness and accountability guide that can aid you in better understanding yourself and with identifying any specific obstacles or challenges that may be in your way. The Notes section can also act as a journal log, where you can input what may have surprised you about your goals, the processes along the way, or anything else you may have found to be significant during your set *"S.M.A.R.T. Goals"* time frames. This is all designed to serve as a reference for your thoughts, feelings, and actions to help guide you toward a better understanding of how and why you operate the ways you do.

(Authors' Note: If you do not wish to write in your copy of this book, or if you need a fresh template, please feel free to download this template separately by visiting www.TiltingTheBalance.com/Templates).

You are now equipped with all of the resources and understandings you should need to properly utilize and complete your *"S.M.A.R.T. Goals"* template.

S.M.A.R.T. GOALS

Done	Item/Goal	Set Date	By Date
☐		(__/ __/ __)	(__/ __/ __)
☐		(__/ __/ __)	(__/ __/ __)
☐		(__/ __/ __)	(__/ __/ __)
☐		(__/ __/ __)	(__/ __/ __)
☐		(__/ __/ __)	(__/ __/ __)
☐		(__/ __/ __)	(__/ __/ __)
☐		(__/ __/ __)	(__/ __/ __)
☐		(__/ __/ __)	(__/ __/ __)
☐		(__/ __/ __)	(__/ __/ __)
☐		(__/ __/ __)	(__/ __/ __)
☐		(__/ __/ __)	(__/ __/ __)
☐		(__/ __/ __)	(__/ __/ __)
☐		(__/ __/ __)	(__/ __/ __)
☐		(__/ __/ __)	(__/ __/ __)
☐		(__/ __/ __)	(__/ __/ __)
☐		(__/ __/ __)	(__/ __/ __)
☐		(__/ __/ __)	(__/ __/ __)
☐		(__/ __/ __)	(__/ __/ __)
☐		(__/ __/ __)	(__/ __/ __)
☐		(__/ __/ __)	(__/ __/ __)
☐		(__/ __/ __)	(__/ __/ __)
☐		(__/ __/ __)	(__/ __/ __)
☐		(__/ __/ __)	(__/ __/ __)
☐		(__/ __/ __)	(__/ __/ __)
☐		(__/ __/ __)	(__/ __/ __)
☐		(__/ __/ __)	(__/ __/ __)
☐		(__/ __/ __)	(__/ __/ __)
☐		(__/ __/ __)	(__/ __/ __)

S.M.A.R.T. GOALS

CHAPTER 14
"THE 3-4-30 CHALLENGE^SM"

"The beginning is the most important part of the work."
– Plato

We are excited to introduce you to our concept of *"The 3-4-30 Challenge^SM."* Since we initially formulated and applied this idea together when first developing *Tilting The Balance*™, *"The 3-4-30 Challenge^SM"* has undergone several transformations in order to have metamorphosed into what it is today.

"The 3-4-30 Challenge^SM" is designed to be a short-term solution to jumpstart your goals for long-term success. Here are the steps:

1. Set your *"S.M.A.R.T Goals."*
2. Find an accountability partner.
3. Determine your challenges together.
4. Routinely meet with your partner as you work to complete set challenges.
5. Repeat or set new challenges together or with a new accountability partner.

We will now explain the premise of these challenges and how you can find your own accountability partners.

After you have completed creating all of your goals into *"S.M.A.R.T. Goals,"* we want you to pick up to three goals (The "3" in *"The 3-4-30 Challenge^SM"*) which you deem to be your highest priorities and want to accomplish the most.

From there, you will choose an accountability partner (preferably someone who wants to pick their own goals and do the challenge with you) and meet with them in person or virtually either four times a week or at least four times per month (The "4" in *"The 3-4-30 Challenge^SM"*), whichever you both prefer.

Once you have found and selected an accountability partner and have each determined your collective goals, you will stick to your challenge for a period of thirty days (The "30" in *"The 3-4-30 Challenge^SM"*) to test, review, and see your results. Bear in mind that if your goals are significant and cannot be fully accomplished in a thirty-day time frame alone, you can set measurable benchmarks to achieve for those goals within the thirty-day span.

After the completion of your thirty-day challenge, you can repeat the exact same goal(s) again for another thirty-day cycle in the event any of them are still applicable, or, you can choose any new goal(s) that you determine to be of the highest priority for you. At this interval as well, you can also choose to work with the same accountability partner or you can opt to select a new one.

If one particular goal you seek to accomplish is extremely challenging for you, then we strongly encourage you to focus solely on that one goal for the thirty-day period.

The main objectives for these challenges are to track your results, review your progress, and celebrate any wins throughout the duration of your set thirty-day time frame. The secondary mission is to discover whether or not the goal(s) you set are even something you still desire to accomplish once the challenge is complete. Oftentimes, it is after we begin to endeavor upon something that we realize it may be much different in reality than how we initially envisioned it to be in our minds, whereas other times, just getting started is all the momentum we may need to project us to the next level.

The role of being an accountability partner is to check in with your partner in consistent, prescheduled intervals to make sure you are sticking with your set challenges.

Again, these meetings can be done in person or virtually via the phone or by other online conference software methods, and should not take more than five to fifteen minutes each (though you can take as long as necessary of course), depending on what the specific goals and tasks consist of. While we highly suggest your accountability partner participates in setting their own individual goals with you, it is not always a mandatory requirement.

The idea behind setting and completing these meetings with a partner is to positively explore together why you may or may not be achieving the goals you set. Your partner is there to help you draw more self-awareness, and can help you celebrate your wins along the way. You can also do the exact same for your partners when they participate in the challenges with you.

The idea is not that this person will complete your goals for you (or you for them, though there may be examples where you can set working goals together), but rather that they will serve as a partner to help enlighten, encourage, and support you. Each partner has their own personal responsibility to take the necessary action steps required to achieve their desired results.

As far as who will make an ideal accountability partner, we recommend doing "*The 3-4-30 Challenge*SM" with anyone who you trust will actively participate with you and most importantly, who you believe will be kind, supportive, trustworthy, reliable, and honest with you. Depending on the nature of your goals, it may also be advisable to select a partner who is knowledgeable about the areas you plan to set goals in. Where sometimes the truth can hurt, it is imperative you partner with someone who is always going to be open, direct, and authentic with you. Constructive feedback can be critical for goal success, and it can be much more easily appreciated when it is delivered in a respectful manner rather than one which may be demeaning or judgmental. This supports why the most ideal accountability partners should be those who are effective communicators that respect you and have a genuine care for you and your success.

You can partner with a family member, a friend, a colleague, business partner, an associate, or anyone who you believe fits the proposed criteria. According to a study performed by The American Society of Training and Development, we have a sixty-five percent greater likelihood of completing a goal when we make a commitment to someone else. That same study also found that if we have specific accountability appointments scheduled with a person, it increases our chances of completing our goal(s) successfully by up to a whopping ninety-five percent!

According to Dr. Rebecca Graber, University of Brighton Senior Lecturer in Psychology, "...friendships are a mechanism supporting the development of psychological resilience in adults." As reflected by Graber's quote, social support can directly contribute to resilience. Research shows that mentally strong people usually have the support systems of friends and family to help them along in their life journeys. Not only does this coincide with the pertinence we explained earlier in having strong *"Family & Friend Relationships,"* it is also exactly why it is so valuable to have accountability partners in your life.

(Authors' Note: To aid you in your search for accountability partners, we have created a special group just for you where you can connect with other like-minded individuals who are looking for accountability partners, too. Please visit our website www.TiltingTheBalance.com/AccountabilityPartners).

Thirty-day challenges can remove the doubt in our minds about whether or not we can actually persist at something long-term. They can also provide a powerful infrastructure that will aid us with more effectively developing new habits from our adjusted actions. Creating new and healthy habits—or breaking old, bad habits—often takes more than thirty days. A thirty-day challenge can get us off to a good start, but scientific research supports that new behaviors become ingrained in our minds after an average of around sixty-six days, though this can also happen in as little as eighteen days or up to two hundred and forty-four days or even more.

Knowing that new habits take time to solidify, you must understand the best way to approach them. Success is not about how many habits you try to change at once, but rather how effectively you can rewire your behavior by focusing on the right ones. Not all goals require habit change. Some are task-based, like completing projects or organizing your personal spaces, while others involve reshaping behaviors that must be reinforced over time. When it comes to habit-based goals, we have learned through experience that trying to change too many at once is generally unsustainable.

The best approach is to focus on no more than one or two major habits at a time. By breaking down your actions into a shorter window, your brain perceives the process as more manageable rather than overwhelming. This shift in perspective helps reframe your thinking, preventing procrastination, reducing resistance to change, and allowing you to build momentum without feeling paralyzed by the size of an overall goal.

When a habit is deeply ingrained, such as a lifelong struggle with food choices as an example, it will likely require your full attention to rewire. When opting to work on multiple habits at once, they should be closely connected, like adjusting diet while increasing hydration, improving sleep and exercise together, or building a morning routine by making your bed and journaling each day. Science supports that humans can only successfully change a limited number of habits at a time, as we only have so much willpower and can easily burn ourselves out. The more habits you simultaneously attempt to change, the less likely they are to stick. You will know a habit has truly been reformed when it no longer feels like an effort to take the action and it becomes second nature. Until then, do not add more to your challenges. The stronger the habit, the longer it may take to change, but lasting change comes from consistency. When you remain focused and trust the process, your commitment to reshaping your habits will create lasting change.

The psychology behind *"The 3-4-30 Challenge*™*"* is that the potential pain of either underperforming or of not completing your thirty-day challenges and letting both yourself and your accountability partner down may most likely help offset the pain and struggles you may experience while eliciting and inculcating your new behaviors. It may also help prompt you to stay motivated. The more difficult you perceive your behavioral changes to be, the more time it may take to transform your new actions into habits.

The design here is to offset the temporary pain associated with making changes with pleasure through experiencing a reward of feeling accomplished when you meet or even exceed your goals. This process will also grant more initial gratification and can help with building positive momentum toward long-term goal success.

Thirty days is just about long enough for you to have an idea of how these new behaviors and actions actually affect your physical, mental, emotional, spiritual, and social life. *"The 3-4-30 Challenge*™*"* can be used as a formula comparable to testing a product for thirty days and then seeing if you actually want to purchase it for good.

We recommend as you think through your challenges that you consider whether you want to add something entirely new to your life, completely eliminate something from your life, or whether or not you want to experiment with setting particular boundaries with certain aspects of life. For example, if you are a cigarette smoker and your goal is to stop smoking altogether, you could structure your thirty-day challenge to stop smoking entirely. If that seems too intense or daunting for a thirty-day duration, you could set some boundaries and limitations to only smoke a certain number of cigarettes per day or only allow yourself to smoke during specific, preset time frames. You could also supplement your nicotine intake with nicotine patches, gum, medications, or other substitutes. Another thing you could do is set a challenge to replace the habit. For example, when you are craving a cigarette, you instead take a drink of water, chew gum, go for a walk, read something, log into a journal, make a phone call, visit a loved one; the list goes on.

We use the example of smoking cigarettes not only to tie in the available options of how to most effectively think through structuring your challenges but also to highlight another important factor you must consider which is how your challenges may affect your physical body, your emotions, your mind, and your spirit. There may be certain changes you want to make which could require consulting a physician or other types of medical providers to ensure you are being safe. This could include activities such as wanting to wean yourself off of existing medications, drugs, substances, or things such as desiring to add more physical exercise or even new or fewer foods into your diet in certain instances. What we are saying is that you need to make sure that you are thinking through setting your challenges with the protection of your personal safety, your physical health, and your mental health being on the forefront of your mind.

The primary purpose of these short-term, thirty-day challenges is to use them to help launch you into making lasting, lifelong changes. Making major life changes is not always easy to do for most of us because the thought and pain of change often makes it difficult for us to even get started. This is why there is such colossal power in using *"The 3-4-30 Challenge*™*"* system as you end up taking action with a reward in mind, as opposed to just taking action on something you may perceive only to be painful or challenging upfront.

The most important wisdom we can bestow upon you is the fact that after your results at the end of your "*3-4-30 Challenge^{SM}*," in the event you do not achieve exactly what you set out to, you must not regard yourself as a failure in any capacity. By simply taking any productive action whatsoever, even through simply shifting your thoughts and focus on embarking upon new positive change and personal development, you are already making virtuous strides toward meaningful self-improvement.

As our friend Grayson Marshall, Jr. so wisely states, "There are only results and restarts." What this means is that no matter what results you achieve, experiencing any results from your challenges that may help you learn and grow should be viewed as victorious in their own right. However, do not misconstrue what we are saying, as this does not mean we encourage you to set these challenges (or any goals for that matter) and not strive to do your absolute best to achieve them just because you are merely thinking about making changes. Where that mentality and approach may stroke your ego, it certainly will not lead you to attaining significant physical results, and it can lead to developing a fallacious habit that it is okay to set goals and not work diligently toward them. It is counterproductive to venture into goal setting with the belief that not meeting your goals is a viable option.

With that being said, if you do happen to make mistakes or have setbacks along the way, we encourage you to make corrections immediately and not allow them to throw off your entire course of action. What we are saying is to do your best and to be honest with yourself about your efforts, about what results you get, or about why you may be experiencing a lack of results in the instances where you may not reach the outcomes you attempted or predicted. When you do your absolute best and fall short of the results you anticipated, there is nothing wrong with resetting, reframing, and restarting.

No matter what outcomes you opt to envision, as long as you do your total best (which is all we can encourage), that is all you can do. Regardless of your results, as long as you are alive and both physically and mentally capable, you can always restart and attempt again.

(Authors' Note: Tony Robbins explains in great detail how our pain and pleasure systems drive behavior in his book Awaken the Giant Within, a resource we highly recommend. He shares a powerful example of a man who quit smoking instantly after his five-year-old daughter, having learned that smoking could cause death, broke down crying and begged him to stop. In that moment, he associated pain with continuing the habit and linked true fulfillment with protecting his daughter and being present in her life.

We again recommend reading The Power of Habit by Charles Duhigg, referenced earlier in the book. His work explores how specific habits influence your daily life at individual, organizational, and societal levels. It is a phenomenal resource for understanding the science behind habit change and offers practical insights for creating lasting, positive routines. Due to its relevance, we adamantly suggest you focus on implementing challenges that help you form consistent, healthy daily habits as part of your long-term growth.

In addition, we suggest reading Atomic Habits by James Clear. He outlines further in-depth strategies for transforming your life through the direct process of habit change. He emphasizes the importance of tracking your habits alongside your goals and explains how to intentionally make your efforts easier to manage by removing points of friction. He also provides downloadable habit-tracking templates to help you stay aware of your progress and strengthen your desire to continue through consistent visual reinforcement. Another helpful concept he introduces is the use of a written contract with your accountability partner, outlining consequences for not following through on your agreed actions. This is certainly an excellent strategy you can apply to your "3-4-30 Challenge℠."

There are a couple more meaningful works we recommend like *Start With Why* by Simon Sinek. Understanding the root of your purpose clarifies motivation, focuses effort, and sustains determination. Complementing this, *The War of Art* by Steven Pressfield exposes the invisible force he calls Resistance, which breeds fear, self-doubt, distraction, procrastination, and perfectionism. Recognizing and confronting this force is essential for forward progress. When your decisions are grounded in purpose and intention, it becomes much easier to produce consistent results.

As we also reviewed earlier in the book, keystone habits play a critical role in shaping how you think, act, and follow through. For a refresher on how to recognize and implement keystone habits that align with your goals, revisit our resource at www.TiltingTheBalance. com/KeystoneHabits.

As you continue your mission of personal development, we urge you to work on developing the habit of completing as many consecutive "3-4-30 Challenges℠" as you realistically can. The awareness and productivity yielded from keeping your goals top of mind, while sharing in accountability and motivation with a partner, are optimized when this practice becomes a routine part of your lifestyle).

(Justin's Note: As this book was just over two years in the making (it took us over five to publish it), I read a book which neither Nick nor I had read prior. The book is titled, *The 12 Week Year* by Brian P. Moran & Michael Lennington. I found it fascinating that neither of us had read their book up to that point, especially due to the amount of similar parallels it shared with what we had already assembled at that time with Tilting The Balance™. The primary reason for mentioning their book is due to their innovative and powerful concept of ditching the formal annualized planning processes and planning only in twelve week intervals. After applying the principles of The 12 Week Year directly into my own life, I found you can also break down your twelve-week goals into smaller thirty-day chunks as we have reviewed in "The 3-4-30 Challenge℠." I highly recommend you read that book, as there is some extremely helpful and beneficial information included throughout their work and on their website, www.12WeekYear.com).

Now, this is where all of the fun (and the work) begins! We are going to review how to properly complete and utilize your template for the "3-4-30 Challenge℠."

This template will help you set a clear path to creating lasting change in your life. It is very similar to the *S.M.A.R.T. Goals* template but with a couple of slight modifications. To help formulate your goals for this challenge, we recommend you use the goals from your completed *S.M.A.R.T. Goals* template which you may perceive to be of the highest priority and the most pertinent to be implemented for your "3-4-30 Challenge℠." Here is how it works:

At the very top of the template where it says *"30-Day Challenge Goals,"* you will add the start date and end date for the thirty-day (or total selected) period you are setting and completing your challenges in.

Example: (Day / Month / Year - Day / Month / Year)

Let's use the example of (01 / 01 / YY - 01 / 30 / YY) as a baseline.

Next, you will fill out the associated date ranges for "Week 1" through (up to) "Week 5." We will continue to use these same date ranges throughout all of the next following examples:

Week 1 (01 / 01 / YY - 01 / 07 / YY)
Week 2 (01 / 08 / YY - 01 / 14 / YY)
Week 3 (01 / 15 / YY - 01 / 21 / YY)
Week 4 (01 / 22 / YY - 01 / 28 / YY)
Week 5 (01 / 29 / YY - 01 / 30 / YY)

(Authors' Note: Here is an important key to understand about these date ranges. If you would like to, you can extend them to go a full month for those months with 31 total days. You can also modify the date ranges so that the first day of your challenge begins on a Monday and the final day ends on a Sunday. This will enable you to begin a brand new "3-4-30 Challenge℠" on the following Monday, though it may shorten or lengthen the challenge by several or more days depending on how you choose to adjust the dates.

We discovered you can make it easier to stay organized when you initially start your challenges on Mondays or if you start and end right at the beginning and end of each month. The key takeaway is, you do not always have to go for the full thirty days so as to make this formula work, though we encourage you not to get into a habit of always cutting your challenges short. The primary goal is to stay consistent by immediately beginning a new "3-4-30 Challenge℠" as soon as the previous one has ended, and that formula can help you stay organized based on which of those approaches you may select).

The next steps are to insert your overall *"3-4-30 Challenge℠"* Goals into the section titled 30-Day Goals. This is where you will insert the overall goal(s) you wish to complete for the time frame you set. You will also use the far right column titled Goal Type to indicate whether or not your goals are Required or Bonus.

As we have suggested, we want you to choose up to at least three Required goals as part of your *"3-4-30 Challenge℠."* If you feel you can handle more, you are welcome to; however, we suggest you do not go overboard. This is why we recommend you use the Bonus goal structure to add goals that you still aspire toward, but if you do not meet them during your challenge while focusing on your Required goals, you will not perceive it to be as problematic. We understand that we stated earlier about how it is not a good habit to set goals you do not wish to work toward accomplishing. The Bonus goal structure is still very much about working to achieve those as well but, not at the expense of your Required goals. Your Required goals are your main priority and Bonus goals are designed to be unmet in the event they may prevent you from focusing on your primary agendas.

*(Authors' Note: As the creators of this content, we spent a rigorous amount of time and hours performing our own "3-4-30 Challenges*SM*." In fact, they have become a routine part of our lifestyles. There was a point in the early phases where we set too many goals for ourselves and found them to be overwhelming. In fact, there was a specific challenge where we actually abandoned several goals mid-challenge and felt great about it! This is what we want you to avoid. Do not put too much pressure on yourself, and advise your accountability partner to keep the same principle in mind. Use the Bonus goal strategy to help offset some of the pressure and keep the primary, core, most important goals as your Required goals. You may even discover that you will automatically accomplish some of the goals you have written down throughout your book while working to achieve your Required goals.*

If you opt to mark a goal as Required, we encourage you to do everything in your power to complete that goal in order to avoid creating the habit that it is okay to not aspire toward achieving the goals you set for yourself. We understand there may always be extenuating circumstances that could prevent you from achieving specific goals, and we can almost guarantee that is going to happen along the way. When it does, become self-aware as to why, reframe your mindset, your approach, reset and start again, or even set new goals when necessary. You are going to learn a great deal about yourself, what works for you, and what does not as you embark upon the journey of routinely performing these challenges. The goal is to do your best and to participate with sheer determination, discipline, and enthusiasm).

Here are some examples:

30-DAY CHALLENGE GOALS (01 / 01 / YY - 01 / 30 / YY)

Done	Item/Goal	Goal Type
☐	Go to the gym a total of three days each week.	Required
☐	Do not eat fried foods or desserts Monday through Friday.	Required
☐	File my taxes.	Required
☐	Go golfing once per week.	Bonus

As you see, your 30-day goals can have recurring benchmarks or they can be a one-time goal that you must achieve during the window of your "3-4-30 Challenge^{SM}." Where there is no right or wrong answer, the mission is to pick goals you believe are of the highest priority for you to achieve. This is where having the self-awareness of your goals being in front of you along with having an accountability partner can aid you in overcoming the obstacle of procrastinating or of not taking appropriate action.

Your *30-Day Challenge Goals* are your primary goals for the duration of your set "3-4-30 Challenge^{SM}."

The next process is to break down your goals into weekly benchmarks. The main initiatives with this breakdown is to either show progress with completion each week, to break down the goals into smaller chunks, to ensure they get done within the allotted time frames, or a combination of all of those objectives. You can use this same formula for any and all of your "S.M.A.R.T. Goals" as well if you want to scale them down into smaller, additional steps.

Here are some examples:

WEEK 1 GOALS (01 / 01 / YY - 01 / 07 / YY)

Done	Item/Goal	Goal Type
☐	Go to the gym a total of three days each week.	Required
☐	Do not eat fried foods or desserts Monday through Friday.	Required
☐	Ensure all of my receipts are updated in a spreadsheet for my taxes.	Required
☐	Go golfing this Thursday.	Bonus

Do you see how each of the main goals were either the exact same or modified based on the specific goals? Let us take a look at other ways you can complete this list going into *Week 2*. Please keep in mind, the overall goal is to get the results you are after. Use the approach toward how you format your goals each week to fit with what works best for **you.**

WEEK 2 GOALS (01 / 08 / YY - 01 / 14 / YY)

Done	Item/Goal	Goal Type
☐	Go to the gym Monday, Wednesday, and Thursday.	Required
☐	Do not eat fried foods or desserts Monday through Friday.	Required
☐	Get all of my financial spreadsheets from my bookkeeper by Friday.	Required
☐	Find a new golf course I've never been to and go Tuesday if I can.	Bonus

Do you notice again how each of the main goals were either the exact same or modified based on the specific goals? Here are some additional ways you can complete this list going into Week 3:

WEEK 3 GOALS (01 / 15 / YY - 01 / 21 / YY)

Done	Item/Goal	Goal Type
☐	Go to the gym Tuesday morning, Wednesday afternoon, and Friday evening.	Required
☐	No fried foods or desserts Monday through Friday.	Required
☐	Send my spreadsheets by Wednesday to my CPA so they can file my taxes.	Required
☐	Go golfing at the new country club I found before the end of the week.	Bonus

That is the gist of it. As you can see, you can be more detailed or keep things less specific with how you choose to adjust each week's processes. The primary mission again is to achieve your goals and to check in with your accountability partner in the time frames we suggested to review either your own or your collective progress together.

Next, as with the *"S.M.A.R.T. Goals"* template, the most integral part of this template is the *Done* checkbox on the left hand frame. This is again where you will check the box or fill it in to mark a goal complete once you achieve it.

There is also a *Notes* section at the end of the template. Similar to the *"S.M.A.R.T. Goals"* template, this time, when you do not complete a goal and get to check or mark the box, both after the end of each week and then at the end of the allotted challenge time frame, we want you to write in the Notes section a brief explanation as to why you were unable to accomplish any individual goal you did not complete, after you have discussed it with your accountability partner first. As with the *"S.M.A.R.T. Goals"* template, we want you to put in as honest of explanations in this section as possible.

The Notes section in this template is similarly designed to serve as a self-awareness guide and a journal log, and this time for both you and your accountability partner if they opt to participate. Of course, when they do, you will want to log your entries in your own templates and your accountability partner will need to log their goals and their notes into their own, separate templates. The next steps are that during your set meetings together you will review and discuss your individual goals and notes, and they will do the same with you for their goals if they are doing the challenge with you. This process will help you better understand your personal thoughts, feelings, and actions, and will guide you toward better understanding how and why you operate the ways you do. Your accountability partner will certainly receive those same exact benefits when they choose to participate with their own goals as well.

The true essence of "*The 3-4-30 Challenge*™" is centered around daily conscious living. It is not about being self-critical if you do not reach a target, or about inflating your ego when you do have personal victories. The power is in gaining the awareness and confidence of how to be at your best while striving to be your best self, and being there for others who may be working with you to do the same. The real transformation happens not just in achieving your goals, but in who you become through the process of consistently showing up for yourself every day.

This is why we encourage making thirty-day challenges a continuous aspect of your routine. As soon as one ends, immediately begin the next. The most productive people in the world operate in structured intervals, turning steady effort into lasting habits that expand into extraordinary results. Whether starting small and building momentum or taking on more ambitious targets, the key is maintaining a pattern of steady growth and self-discovery. Each day becomes an opportunity to refine your approach while staying connected with supportive partners throughout your journey.

(Authors' Note: If you do not wish to write in your copy of this book, or if you need a fresh template, please feel free to download this template separately by visiting www.TiltingTheBalance.com/Templates).

You are now equipped with all of the resources and understandings you need to properly set, conduct, and most effectively find your accountability partners for your own "*3-4-30 Challenge*™."

"THE 3-4-30 CHALLENGE℠"

Done	Item/Goal	Goal Type
☐		
☐		
☐		
☐		
☐		
	Week 1 (__ / __ / __ - __ / __ / __)	
☐		
☐		
☐		
☐		
☐		

Done	Item/Goal	Goal Type
	"THE 3-4-30 CHALLENGE℠"	
	Item/Goal	Goal Type
	Week 2 (__/__/ __ -__/__/ __)	
☐		
☐		
☐		
☐		
☐		
	Week 3 (__/__/ __ -__/__/ __)	
☐		
☐		
☐		
☐		
☐		

Done	Item/Goal	Goal Type
	"THE 3-4-30 CHALLENGE^{SM}"	
	Week 4 (__/__/__-__/__/__)	
☐		
☐		
☐		
☐		
☐		
	Week 5 (__/__/__-__/__/__)	
☐		
☐		
☐		
☐		
☐		

"THE 3-4-30 CHALLENGE^{SM}"

"THE 3-4-30 CHALLENGE^{SM}"

Notes:

CHAPTER 15
DREAMSCAPING

"Thoughts become things. If you see it in your mind, you will hold it in your hand."
— Bob Proctor

We reviewed prior the power of visualization and our body's "Reticular Activating System." Since we understand how our thoughts and feelings influence our subconscious minds to focus on what we find to be relevant and important, then is it not more advantageous to adopt the belief that we have some level of control to create our own circumstances, as opposed to only having the ability to merely react to them?

You see, we tend to build things in our lives from sets of plans, such as toys, furniture, homes, buildings, vehicles, airplanes, etc., yet most of us do not have plans for exactly how we want to construct our perfect realities, nor do we especially have clear ideas of what our ideal realities would look and feel like.

We have an exercise that will help you form a clear vision of what your dream life would actually look and feel like in the event it were already your reality. Introduced to us in Jeff Lerner's ENTRE Institute, harnessing the powers of your mind, visualization, and quantum mechanics, Dreamscaping is an exceptionally powerful exercise that will help you conjure and actualize your dreams and desires.

The premise of Dreamscaping is to write down what your life would look like in the event all things were one-hundred-percent perfect, and with our spin on the exercise, we want you to categorize everything within each area of *"The 10 Categories of Life."*

The key principle is to not worry about where you are **now** but rather to only focus on where you **dream** to be within each area of your life. You will think through what you want your days to look like, your lifestyle, your experiences, your body, your relationships, your career, and what legacy you want to leave behind.

As you consider what your dream life will look like in each category of life in the present tense, as if you have already accomplished your goals and dreams ahead of having lived out the actual experiences, you are going to write them down, preferably physically and using the template we provide for this exercise. From there, the goal is to review your dream life on a regular basis and utilize it as an aid in visualization techniques, thinking with the end in mind and working to feel the experiences in as much detail as possible as if the events or circumstances you are imagining are occurring in real time. We also want you to experience the feelings of gratitude, feeling thankful and appreciative, giving thanks as if you have already received what you want ahead of the physical experience.

We do not want you to worry about **how** you will create these results and only want you to use this exercise as a way to identify exactly **what** it is that you want. Be sure to always use a present tense for each item you add, to be as specific and detailed as possible, and to not be afraid to include as many items to your list as you see fit.

Here is the framework for completing the template we have provided you with for this exercise:

THE SELF, CORE VALUES, & BELIEF SYSTEMS

If everything was perfect, how would you feel about yourself? What are some of the beliefs you would have about yourself? How would you feel about the ways you hold yourself accountable? What would you be grateful for and what would your routines look like? Who would be your social influences or how would you be an influence yourself?

This is where you are going to contemplate all of the aspects of *"The 10 Fundamentals of Self-Love"* and can consider writing statements like this:

"I am always grateful for all of the amazing blessings I have"

"I am always positive and am confident in myself and my abilities"

"I always achieve my goals and hold myself super accountable for everything I say and do"

"I always follow healthy and productive routines"

"I am always physically, mentally, emotionally, and spiritually healthy and fulfilled"

As you can see, some of the statements you may create in this exercise can even be utilized as effective affirmations.

PERSONAL TASKS

Consider what your perfect life would look like if all of your personal tasks were handled, and imagine how you would feel about yourself and your personal tasks. What qualities would you possess and what services might you have available for you? Here are some examples:

"My home, vehicles, and all of my personal belongings are always extremely organized. I have services who clean my home, vehicles, and do my laundry and landscaping on a weekly basis."

As you continue this exercise, you can always factor in *"The Self, Core Values, & Belief Systems"* and how you would believe your life would be perfect in each category. For example:

"I am always extremely efficient and organized with all of my personal tasks"

"I am always in control of my personal tasks"

PHYSICAL FITNESS & MENTAL WELLNESS

What would your perfect life look like if you were in the most optimal physical and mental condition you desire to be in? What type of body would you have? What kind of mental state would you want to reside in? How would you want to feel about yourself physically and mentally? Consider these examples:

"I am in prime physical condition with six pack abs and clearly defined muscles"

"I am always feeling happy and energetic"

"Exercise is always an integral aspect of my weekly routine"

"I always eat organic foods, use healthy products, and have a nutritious, balanced diet"

"I am free of anxiety and do not stress about the small things"

HOBBIES, PASSIONS, & INTERESTS

What would your perfect life look like if you were fulfilled by all of your hobbies, passions, and interests? What types of activities are you doing for fun? Where are you traveling and what memories are you creating? What new experiences are you having? What material possessions do you own? Some examples can include:

"I always go golfing a minimum of once per week"

"I own specific boats or I am a member of a specific boat club"

"I have the ability to travel wherever I want, whenever I want"

"I own homes or properties in specific cities or areas"

"I own material possessions such as specific powersports, recreational vehicles, clothing, collectibles, etc."

FAMILY & FRIEND RELATIONSHIPS

What would your life be like if all of your family and friend relationships were perfectly how you wanted them to be? Who exactly are you spending time with? What types of activities are you doing together? How do you feel about these relationships? Some examples are:

"I am always able to spend time communicating or visiting with the family and friends I love and care about"

"My family and friends are always treating me with love, respect, and appreciation"

"I am always able to help my family and friends with any financial resources they may need"

"I am always easily making new friends with amazing people"

"I am always taking my family and friends on vacations and providing them with new experiences at my financial expense"

ROMANTIC RELATIONSHIPS

This is where we are going to visualize everything we are looking for in our romantic relationships. Do you know what kind of partner you are looking for? What do they look like or how do they make you feel? Do you already have someone in mind? Are you wanting improvements or to make changes in existing romantic relationships? Are there specific romantic experiences you are seeking? Remember, these things do not have to be real yet in order for you to dream of them:

"My partner and I always communicate effectively and lovingly together"

"My partner always loves, respects, supports, and seeks to understand me"

"My partner and I always share equally in our duties and responsibilities to ourselves, each other, and our family"

"I have beautiful children with an amazing partner"

"I consistently go on date nights every week and/or am always experiencing the affection and company of multiple partners"

SPIRITUALITY

What does your life look like if it were spiritually fulfilled and perfect? Where do you want to be and how do you want to feel spiritually? How do you feel in your faith and what specific actions are you taking to further develop it? Are you attending church, temple, synagogue or other types of religious functions? Are there specific spiritual experiences you are having or practices you are following? Consider these examples:

"I always meditate, recite affirmations, and perform gratitude and visualization techniques every day"

"I always trust in my faith, feeling enlightened, positive, and free of stress"

"I regularly attend religious events with my family"

"I always feel close to and have an amazing relationship with God"

"I always read books and review content that spiritually uplifts me"

CHARITABLE GIVING

Imagine the fulfillment you would feel and the ways you would give if everything was perfect. How much money, time, or resources are you giving and to whom are you giving to? How exactly would you feel about giving? What specific differences would you be making and how? Here are some examples:

"I always give ten percent of my annual earnings to specific charities"

"I always volunteer my time once per week for a specific organization"

"I own and operate my own charity that serves a specific cause I care about"

"I always have all of the means I need to enable me to donate as much time, money, and resources as I want"

"I always feel amazing when I donate my time and money to meaningful purposes and causes"

Remember, it is up to you to decide who you specifically want to give to and how you want to give to them.

FINANCIAL RESPONSIBILITIES

This section is what your life would look like if everything was financially perfect. How and what would you be doing financially and how would you feel about your financial positions? Are you debt free? How much money do you have? Do you have a wide range of investments and, if so, what are they? There are a myriad of examples you can consider:

"I have a net worth of ten million dollars and net over one hundred thousand dollars annually"

"I always save over fifty percent of my income and am completely debt free"

"I am fully retired and live entirely off of interest from specific investments"

"I am always financially abundant and get to do whatever I want to with my financial wealth"

"I am on the Forbes list of the wealthiest people in the world"

BUSINESS & CAREER OBJECTIVES

Here, we are visualizing what your perfect business and career life looks like. Do you own your own business? Are you the CEO of a company? Do you have the dream job you have always wanted? Do you have the freedoms, responsibilities, assets, or benefits associated with the career you have always wanted? Think through these examples:

"I always have plenty of time to do what I love outside of work"

"I founded and own a company that was featured in Success Magazine"

"I am a New York Times Best Selling Author"

"I am an award-winning, hall-of-fame-inducted athlete"

"I have my dream job and love going to work"

Whatever you dream of accomplishing in the business world, the only limitations are most likely the ones you create for yourself.

There you have it. As you can see, the possibilities are virtually endless. With some brainstorming and critical thinking, you can incorporate all of the end results you dream of in this exercise and utilize them as extremely powerful visualization and affirmation techniques. The goal is to revisit the statements you create through the Dreamscaping exercise on a daily basis, preferably making it a part of both your morning and evening routines. As we reviewed prior in the "Visualizations" chapter:

"The goal is to imagine yourself in a reality which you desire yourself to be. Not only do you need to imagine yourself in that reality, you also must feel what it would feel like to be in that reality, as we suggested you do earlier in this chapter to harness the power of affirmations. The more clear and detailed you are in your visual realities and the more you are able to feel them to be real, the more viable chances you have of manifesting your visualizations into your actual physical reality."

By having a clear idea and strong visualization of your goals and dreams, and through reviewing them on a regular and consistent basis, you are constantly calling awareness to them, impressing them upon your subconscious mind, and putting them out into the universe to be later drawn back into your physical reality.

We also want to note, if any of your dreams change, that is okay, you can always re-write them and make whatever changes you wish, whenever you wish. We hope you enjoyed this exercise and that you utilize it to help bring your dream life into fruition.

(Authors' Note: We have reviewed the powers and differences of the conscious versus the subconscious mind, and how important it is to feel the feelings of having our dreams accomplished before actually experiencing them coming true in our physical realities. Once you have completed your Dreamscaping exercise, we have assembled some powerful content that will aid you in further visualizing your Dreamscaping visions on a much deeper and more substantial level. We will share some effective visualization techniques that will support you in further feeling as if all of your dreams have already been accomplished.

Please visit www.TiltingTheBalance.com/VisionGazing to learn more about "VisionGazing[SM]*," our immersive, multi-sensory approach to bringing your future into* *focus. We also have additional tools to help you most effectively create a dream board that supports your vision. Visit www.TiltingTheBalance.com/DreamBoard to access those resources).*

(Authors' Note: If you do not wish to write in your copy of this book, or if you need a fresh template, please feel free to download this template separately by visiting www.TiltingTheBalance.com/Templates).

You are now equipped with everything you need to properly complete your "Dreamscaping" template.

DREAMSCAPING

YOURSELF, CORE VALUES, & BELIEF SYSTEMS

PERSONAL TASKS

PHYSICAL FITNESS & MENTAL WELLNESS

HOBBIES, PASSIONS, & INTERESTS

FAMILY & FRIEND RELATIONSHIPS

ROMANTIC RELATIONSHIPS

DREAMSCAPING

SPIRITUALITY

CHARITABLE GIVING

FINANCIAL RESPONSIBILITIES

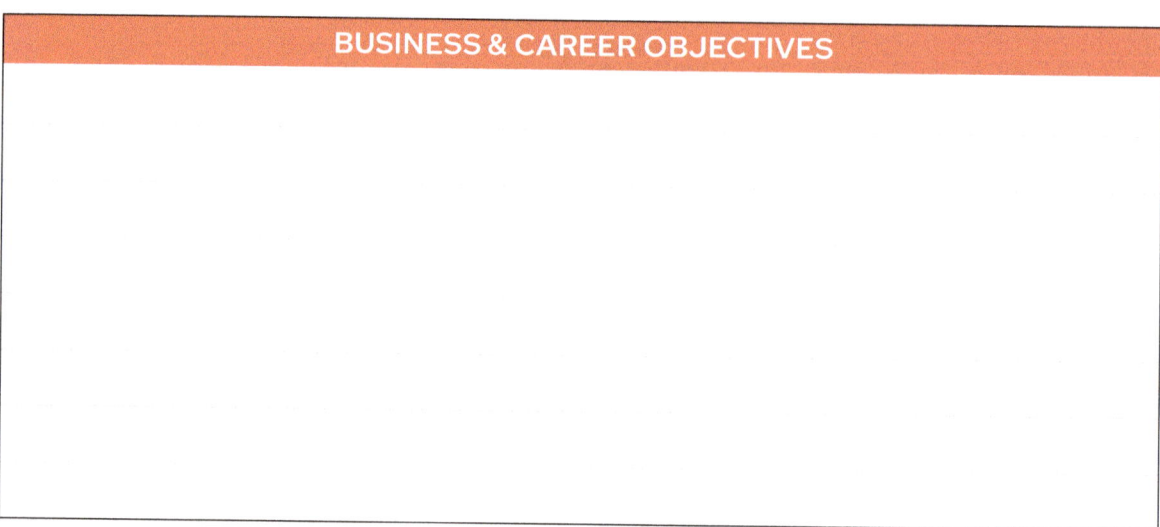

BUSINESS & CAREER OBJECTIVES

DREAMSCAPING

CONCLUSION

"It's better to do less than you hoped than nothing at all."
— James Clear

We commend and congratulate you for reading *Tilting The Balance*™ in its entirety. We hope you have found it to be informative, inspirational, and empowering. By reaching the end of this book, you have taken significant steps toward understanding yourself and designing a life that aligns with your true desires. This is not just about finishing a book; it is about starting new and exciting chapters in your own life.

As you focus on *"The 10 Categories of Life"* and embrace *"The 10 Fundamentals of Self-Love,"* remember that each category offers a wealth of insights and strategies that can be adapted to your unique circumstances and goals. By applying the principles and techniques outlined in this book, you can create positive change across every area of your life.

To ensure the lessons from *Tilting The Balance*™ are deeply ingrained, we encourage you to reread this book and to review your exercises regularly. In 1885, German psychologist Hermann Ebbinghaus published "The Forgetting Curve," a model demonstrating how quickly we forget new information. According to his research, we lose approximately forty percent of new memories within the first twenty minutes, fifty percent after an hour, sixty percent after a day, and seventy percent after two days. After a month, we retain only about twenty percent of the original information we initially obtained. By repeatedly engaging with the content in this book, you can counteract this natural forgetting process and better internalize the key principles and strategies for creating lasting success. The exercises in this book are also most effective when practiced frequently.

For complete comprehension and internalization of the principles in this book, we want to provide clear instructions on how to use the various templates and exercises it contains. *"The Mind Dump"* exercise is most effective when performed regularly to reduce mental clutter and enhance focus. We recommend making it a weekly habit to revisit previous *"Mind Dumps."* This allows tracking of progress, identification of lingering tasks, and necessary adjustments.

At the start of each month or right before starting a new *"The 3-4-30 Challenge*™,*"* create a fresh "Mind Dump" to clear residual mental clutter and approach goals with a renewed perspective. During high-stress periods or when feeling overwhelmed, consider using *"The Mind Dump"* exercise daily to regain clarity and focus. This practice helps you adapt to immediate challenges while keeping long-term priorities in mind. We encourage adapting this frequency to your individual needs and using it anytime mental overload occurs.

Equally important is revisiting all other templates and exercises in this book with consistency and intention. Life is dynamic, and your goals, priorities, and dreams will naturally evolve over time. To stay aligned with your aspirations and to make continual meaningful progress, we recommend revisiting templates from *"The 10 Categories of Life"* at least once every one to two weeks. This allows evaluation of current goals, progress tracking, and small adjustments as needed. Regular reviews ensure connection to what matters most while maintaining focus and organization.

In addition to weekly or bi-weekly reviews, we encourage completely redoing your templates using fresh ones at least once every three months. Quarterly reassessments provide the opportunity to reflect on how your circumstances and priorities may have shifted. By restarting, new visions can be contrasted with your prior ones. This ensures all of your goals remain relevant, inspiring, and aligned with the person you are striving to become. This balance of regular reviews and quarterly resets helps maintain adaptability and motivation, no matter what challenges life may present.

As templates are reviewed, it is essential to regularly transform your ideas into *"S.M.A.R.T. Goals."* We recommend doing this as part of your ongoing template reviews. By transforming broader ideas into actionable steps, progress becomes tangible and measurable, ensuring steady momentum toward your aspirations.

The *"Assessing Current Life Balance: The 10 Categories Exercise"* is another vital tool to help determine where you presently stand in all areas of life. Revisit this exercise anytime feeling "off" without understanding why, and especially before starting a new *"3-4-30 Challenge*SM.*"* By periodically reassessing your life balance, areas experiencing dissatisfaction can be pinpointed and necessary adjustments can immediately be made to realign focus. This ensures that each challenge undertaken is purposeful and targeted toward the areas of life that need the most care and attention.

One of the most powerful components of this system is the *"The 3-4-30 Challenge*SM,*"* and we urge you to commit to starting a new challenge every thirty days. Get into the routine of participating in these like clockwork, as these challenges are designed to create consistent progress and build lasting habits. Each challenge allows the opportunity to set new goals and focus on measurable outcomes that propel forward momentum. By habitually completing and beginning new challenges every thirty days, growth can become a regular and sustainable part of your life. It also reinforces awareness, discipline, and accountability, helping build trust and confidence in yourself and your abilities to follow through on commitments. Over time, it cultivates a growth and action-oriented mindset, allowing obstacles to be seen as opportunities for improvement rather than setbacks.

Continuous participation in *"The 3-4-30 Challenge*SM"* will shift your mindset to being proactive rather than reactive, enabling more thoughtful responses to situations instead of impulsive reactions. They also provide clarity and focus, and can aid you in prioritizing what truly matters while letting go of negativity and distractions. By regularly reflecting on progress, areas of excellence can be uncovered and areas needing more attention or effort can be recognized. This balanced self-awareness empowers ongoing refinement of your approach, ensuring that each challenge brings you one step closer to the life you desire most.

Another key to success with our system is to revisit your Dreamscaping exercise often in order to utilize it as a powerful visualization tool. Reflecting on your Dreamscaping exercises at least once a month keeps your long-term vision clear and top of mind. This practice ensures you stay connected with your goals and allows you to adjust as growth occurs, keeping you aligned with any evolving aspirations.

Earlier in the book, we guided you to resources for crafting a Chief Aim Statement, as inspired by Napoleon Hill's Think and Grow Rich. This may be one of the most powerful practices to integrate with our system, as it provides a clear mental picture of who you want to be and the life you want to create. By pairing this vision with your Dreamscaping exercises, it can be integrated into a routine visualization ritual that reinforces your goals while magnifying your ability to achieve them.

Beyond monthly reviews, we encourage completely redoing Dreamscaping exercises at least every six months or as often as once per quarter. Aligning this practice with your quarterly template revisions allows you to reflect on your progress and to refine and adapt any long-term goals. By refreshing your Dreamscaping exercise every three to six months, you can stay proactive in shaping objectives that best fit the life you want to build and support the person you want to become.

By integrating all of these practices into your routine, you can create a dynamic system for ongoing personal growth and fulfillment. Always remember, this process is about progress, not perfection. Winning and achieving results can be exhilarating, but it is equally important to embrace shortcomings gracefully, seeing them not as setbacks but as valuable opportunities to learn, grow, and optimize your approach.

Adjust your strategies as needed, stay consistent, and trust in the power of the resources you have gained. Set meaningful goals, work diligently to accomplish them, and design the life that aligns with your dreams. It is up to you to ensure you are "tilting the balance" in your daily life.

As you implement these practices, we remind you to enjoy the journey. Make the most of your time, cherish the meaningful moments, and embrace as many fun and enriching experiences as possible along the way.

This leads us to another crucial concept. There is a profound difference between taking control of life and learning to let go. Life is a balancing act of making things happen and allowing them to do so. We are both the sculptor and the clay, creating our lives while being shaped by forces beyond our grasp. This is the power of surrender.

Surrendering is not about being passive or careless. It is the conscious act of releasing our attachments to outcomes and our own personal preferences while still showing up with consistent effort, clarity, and intention. There is an intrinsic balance in being purposeful and in how life sometimes unfolds for reasons beyond our comprehension. Sometimes we meet deadlines, while others we meet dead ends.

Think back to times when a desired outcome did not go according to plan. Maybe a relationship was lost, or it was an opportunity that you wanted. Where it may have left you feeling negative at the time of its occurrence, and maybe even for some time afterwards, after days, weeks, months, or even years later, there was likely an epiphany that one day followed where it became clear how redirection occurred to point you toward something better, be it a deeper relationship, a more fulfilling career, or another opportunity that fit more ideally than what we thought could have been possible.

We live in a culture that often glorifies constant hustle and visible success, and tend to trust those who appear to have what we want. The physique, the money, the materials. Whatever we feel we lack or want more of. What cannot be measured though is happiness and fulfillment. Inner peace. This is the wealth we urge you to strive for. Focus primarily on nurturing your mind, body, and spirit, and on supporting others in their own well-being. The rest of what you want can be amassed as a byproduct.

By doing this, you can find the deepest inner faith that care will be received in return. Move at a sustainable pace through life, focus on your own personal growth and development rather than comparing yourself or your progress to others, and trust in the process. Enjoy the journey, and stay safe and kind along the way.

True surrender allows us to flow with life rather than against it. We must master the art of rolling with the punches, bending with the wind, and floating in the current instead of exhausting ourselves fighting against it all. As Tony Robbins reminds us, "life is not happening to us, but rather it's always happening for us." When we stop trying to control every detail, we often find that life opens doors we never could see before.

Coming back full circle, this does not mean we abandon our goals or lose sight of our grandest visions. *Tilting The Balance*™ is built around making deliberate, conscious efforts. We must make meaningful choices, set impactful goals, and take consistent action. However, we also ask you to hold that discipline in equipoise with trust. True peace often follows when we pursue our best life with energy while releasing the need to cling to how or when results must arrive.

As so many prolific authors such as Michael Singer, Eckhart Tolle, Dr. Joe Dispenza teach, so much of our suffering comes from trying to control what we cannot. When we loosen our grip, we gain freedom. When we surrender, we discover space for joy, creativity, and unexpected opportunities. This marks the end of our philosophical exploration; for now.

Above all else, we want everyone to believe in their ability to achieve anything they set their mind to. Everyone deserves to live the life of their dreams, and we are here to provide support every step of the way. This is our reminder that you do not have to go after your goals alone. Whether you are seeking guidance on setting actionable goals, overcoming obstacles, or refining strategies to manage your operations more effectively, our coaching services are custom-tailored to meet you where you are. Together, we will help you clarify your purpose, sharpen your vision, and achieve the life you have always imagined.

If you choose to contact us, we are dedicated to helping you work toward your goals directly. Learn more about our coaching services by visiting www.TiltingTheBalance.com/LiveLearning.

We also encourage you to join our community of like-minded individuals and to connect with others striving to live their best lives today by visiting www.TiltingTheBalance.com/AccountabilityPartners.

Lastly, we would love to learn about how *Tilting The Balance*™ has impacted your life. If this book helps you to create a personal breakthrough, start a meaningful project, or if you change the lives of others because of what you learn here, please share it in any way possible. Tag us online, use our dedicated hashtag #TTB4E (Tilting The Balance For Everyone), or contact us directly at www.TiltingTheBalance.com/ContactUs to share your experiences.

We extend our heartfelt thanks for your time, engagement, and trust in our work, and we wish you continued success on your journey toward a balanced and fulfilling life.

With All of Our Support and Gratitude,

Justin M. Bullock & Nicolas A. Houpt

(Authors' Note: Be sure also to visit our website regularly to explore an abundance of new and updated content, templates, and cutting-edge resources. Feel free to share it with others and if you know someone who could benefit from our work, you can purchase a copy for them or direct them to our website at www.TiltingTheBalance.com/BuyNow to obtain one).

RECOMMENDED READING

(Author's Note: To find a full list of our recommended reading for viewing or purchase please visit www.TiltingTheBalance.com/OurFavoriteBooks).

CO-AUTHOR EPILOGUE

– Justin M. Bullock

Thank you for investing your time in this journey with us. We spent over five years refining this work and sincerely hope this book has provided meaningful value to your life. The concept for *Tilting The Balance*™ emerged from inspiration drawn particularly from Jeff Olson's The Slight Edge and Gary Keller and Jay Papasan's The One Thing. The latter sparked the foundation for our *"10 Categories of Life"* framework and other transformative concepts that profoundly shaped my perspective.

My immersion in books and materials on personal and professional development, quantum physics, and metaphysics, combined with reflection on my own experiences, planted the seeds for this book. However, its true evolution began with the inspired thought that led to that pivotal call to Nick Houpt on December, 26, 2019. Since we were both immersed in similar personal development journeys yet struggling to achieve our desired results, why not combine our energies? I proposed we set specific goals, embark on a thirty-day process together, meet weekly to track our progress, and document our journey in a book. Neither one of us could have imagined how that single moment would ultimately lead us creating the system of *Tilting The Balance*™. What began as a simple idea evolved into a life-changing system beyond our wildest expectations.

Since Nick immediately embraced the vision early after that phone conversation, we had launched into action right after the holidays. While our initial efforts yielded promising outcomes, we quickly discovered that maintaining consistency proved difficult during the early phases of our thirty-day challenges.

Many months of trial and error led us to the truth that lasting change materializes only when someone is truly prepared to prioritize it. As we gained momentum and refined our approach, we enlisted one of my mentees, Gokul Madathil, to help transform our concepts into coherent written form. His exceptional organizational and writing skills proved instrumental in making this book possible. Nick and I will forever remain grateful for his invaluable contributions.

As we began to further refine our first draft, we discovered how breaking life into distinct categories offered us a clear and powerful way to assess our circumstances and priorities. It simplified our lives, their complexities, and brought us an understanding that we never had before. With that new perspective, we quickly recognized the profound impact of clarity when integrated with accountability in our early thirty-day trials. As we progressed together, successes inspired us, and setbacks strengthened our resilience while increasing our self-awareness. Every experiment, whether a triumph or a struggle, offered us an opportunity to learn, grow, and improve.

Eventually, we framed and structured the thirty-day period as the *"3-4-30 Challenge*SM*."* My first ones primarily began with focusing on health improvements. Through intermittent fasting, eliminating processed foods and sugars, maintaining a low-carb diet with consistent exercise, and even ensuring I flossed my teeth twice daily, I witnessed encouraging results.

However, over five consecutive years of personally experimenting with *"The 3-4-30 Challenge*SM*"* has revealed fundamental principles that can rapidly enhance implementation of this practice. The first insight is that most habits, especially deeply rooted ones, require significantly longer than thirty days to fully transform. My direct experiences with dietary habits illustrate this truth. Despite achieving remarkable weight loss during thirty-day focused challenges (on more than one occasion), I still found myself encountering ongoing fluctuations, all stemming from deeply ingrained childhood behaviors.

It took me considerable time to realize why that was, and to conclude that my health and weight management required ongoing attention and consistent effort. However, due to the formula of implementing ongoing awareness and execution, this realization led me to ensure that I am always participating in a *"3-4-30 Challenge*SM*,"* and most especially those with an emphasis on my physical health.

While some endeavors easily become new habits through minor repetition, not all will. This is why the best path to transformation is permanent participation in a *"3-4-30 Challenge*SM*."* By always aiming to reach new heights and pairing your work with ongoing accountability, this approach creates powerful synergy between immediate achievements and long-term transformation, maintaining momentum while systematically reshaping ingrained beliefs. The high measures of awareness it creates and the sense of responsibility that it promotes can drive immediate accomplishments. It is precisely the recipe that leads to lasting change and to the reformation or establishment of new habits in areas needing improvement.

Successfully implementing *"The 3-4-30 Challenge*SM*"* on a consecutive basis does require a delicate balancing act. The best strategy is to address as many of the utmost priority areas needing change simultaneously, without overwhelming yourself with too many objectives at once. When possible, it is also critical to identify leverage points where you can work on changes that have the ability to drastically improve several life areas at once. As you work toward changing specific behaviors, for any that require intense discipline, the key is to repeat those same challenges until those actions become second nature. Success becomes evident when confidence and results stem automatically, and you no longer feel the need to include those objectives in your challenges.

Be cautious though, as sometimes, you can make progress in an area and think you found mastery only to find yourself later slipping back into prior patterns of behavior. If this does occur, simply revisit your same earlier approaches that were centered around those initiatives until your corrective repeat actions solidify further. Eventually, you can fully rewire your thoughts and actions. If an objective is absolutely imperative enough, you can always reintroduce a prior goal amidst an active *"3-4-30 Challenge*SM*,"* as long as it does not interfere with your current goals or if you are able to adequately adjust them as needed to ensure proper optimization. As you repeat processes, reframe thinking, behaviors, and habits, you can apply the same formula to build better patterns in other areas. Focus intently on goals, master the most pertinent actions and habits through repetition, then move forward to the next most priority areas. By staying intentional and persistent in this manner, you can overcome obstacles and achieve meaningful, lasting personal success.

My goal here in closing is to give you as much sound advice as I can. Another (and perhaps the most crucial) principle is the power of your social influences. Surrounding yourself with people who support your endeavors, keep you on track, share in your struggles, and celebrate your wins can make a tremendous difference in reaching your objectives. Choosing the right people who share a growth mindset, free of envy, jealousy, negativity, and cynicism, who love and support you, and who will always be honest and direct is critical.

Through my own evolution, I have reached a fundamental conclusion that we covered in the beginning of this book. There are many buzz words used in the personal development space about "discipline," "commitment," and "motivation." However, I have found that once you have uncovered your purpose and achieved an extreme level of focus and clarity, motivation, commitment, and discipline emerge more naturally as byproducts. Having a deep sense of purpose drives disciplined action, which promotes consistency, and continual effort is exactly what drives progress and meaningful results.

When you know the true why behind your main initiatives, the answers for what to do and how to do it tend to reveal themselves. Combining this understanding with the wisdom from this book will help maximize your impact. Therefore, if you have not, I strongly encourage you to take the time to develop your Chief Aim Statement.

Another valuable lesson came from two of my mentors, both multimillionaires with vastly different personalities. As I struggled throughout the majority of my entrepreneurial journey to maintain traction at times due to overextending myself, at one low point, I remember asking them what differentiated their outcomes from my approach, and their answers were identical. They both separately emphasized the same exact principle about concentrating on building one bridge at a time when it comes to businesses, and this insight certainly applies to all other areas of life. Their key to success was to concentrate solely in one area first, establish it fully, then moving to the next. Build each bridge plank by plank with purpose and efficiency before starting another. Many people begin working toward one objective, only to get distracted by another opportunity and abandon their progress, creating a cycle of incomplete action. This scattered approach rarely yields what we are after.

This principle of singular focus has become a way of life for me, and has significantly impacted my own journey in the most positive ways. I share these insights to emphasize that lasting transformation takes purpose, time, and continuous effort. Long-term change typically does not happen overnight. It is a process of learning, evolving, seeking qualified support, and moving forward one step at a time. Enjoying the journey along the way is just as important, if not more so, than arriving at your destinations. The reality is that life is short and fragile, and you may not ever reach all of your objectives to begin with. Therefore, why not enjoy yourself as much as possible along the way? This serves as a powerful reminder to cherish all of life's moments and to avoid putting so much pressure on yourself that you rush yourself through it. If you want a great visual and emotional example of this principle, I highly recommend watching the movie Click with Adam Sandler if you have not seen it.

I can humbly admit that I once fell into the trap of hyper-focus that was highlighted in that film, prioritizing business goals at the expense of relationships and personal well-being. That imbalance led to burnout and one of the darkest periods of my life. Yet, it was through that pain, and embracing the principles we have outlined in this book, that I discovered a newfound understanding of balance and joy. Today, I make it a priority to schedule healthy, engaging, and fulfilling activities every week, alongside my professional pursuits. If not for those experiences, I would not be equipped with the experience to be an effective coach, have the love for helping others that I do, and I certainly do not believe you would be reading this now, as *Tilting The Balance*™ would most likely not exist.

All of the lessons I have learned throughout the development of this book taught me something deeper about how life actually works. I cannot explain how many experiences I have had that were happenstance and worked out more favorably than I could have ever anticipated, right after going through something that felt so devastating at the time. When I learned to accept that everything will work out the way it is supposed to, and as long as I do my part with balancing my actions paired with letting go of trying to control everything, that is where my life became magical. It is so easy to get caught up and compare our value with the general consensus of what success means. Most people think it is about having all of the material things.

We are apt to be overly trusting of the people that have all of the physique, the money, the stuff. I am here to tell you; that is not real wealth, and not all of these individuals have everything we might think they do. I do not care how you look physically or how much your net worth is. You cannot buy inner peace or true fulfillment. You cannot buy being a genuinely good person to yourself and others. You cannot own deep, authentically loving relationships, or a truly healthy mind, body, or spirit. You always have to work for these aspects of life, and these are the blessings to cherish and appreciate most.

This understanding of what matters most directly shapes how I work with others. My commitment to you is that I will only ever work to teach you what I know. Where I am human and will never be perfect, it is forever my goal to live by example, to do the right thing when no one is watching, and to remain committed to being at my best and doing my best to help inspire, encourage, and empower you to be at yours.

The entire process of developing *Tilting The Balance*™ has shown me that our system is a powerful method for creating lasting change. I have overcome lifelong addictions, insecurities, and completely revolutionized my thinking in ways that are still somewhat incomprehensible. I am confident that by applying these principles we have taught you throughout this book, adopting the mindsets we have shared, and through dedicating yourself to taking massive action while following the steps, you can also achieve personal success beyond what you may currently imagine is even possible.

Through my coaching, I primarily help others achieve desired results in goal-setting, mindset, ongoing accountability, personal and romantic relationships, launching and scaling businesses, maximizing overall health, and real estate investing. Rather than the intensive syndication work I previously described, I now maintain a balanced approach to real estate that aligns with the principles in this book, and remain open to select partnerships and opportunities, especially for those in Northeast Florida. However I can be a resource for you, the reality is, my dreams do not come true unless yours do. If you would like to connect with me directly for any purpose, to share a cause, or discuss potential collaborations, please send me a correspondence by visiting www. TiltingTheBalance.com/ContactUs. I look forward to hearing from you and supporting you in your endeavors.

Thank you for reading *Tilting The Balance*™. Writing this book has been a dream come true, and my greatest hope is that it inspires you to pursue and achieve your own dreams. I wish you a life filled with love, happiness, prosperity, and success.

With Gratitude,

Justin M. Bullock

CO-AUTHOR EPILOGUE

– Nicolas A. Houpt

When we began writing this book, I believed countless people, myself included, could benefit from its insights. However, until it was finished, I did not fully realize the true impact it could have on others. I have yet to find another book that combines a step-by-step plan for achieving one's true desires with exercises that help you explore your mind, body, and soul to uncover what those desires truly are. Not to mention that you can physically write in it to organize and map out your goals and life.

The steps outlined in this book may not always be easy, but they are straightforward and can lead to dramatic changes in your life if applied consistently. My life is completely different from when we first started writing this book. At that time, I was in an entirely different place and, really, an entirely different person. I was single, living alone, neglecting my health, out of shape, and feeling unfulfilled in my career, spirituality, and life overall. My savings and investments were minimal, and, to be completely honest, I was struggling with alcohol abuse, which left me deeply unhappy with myself.

Fast forward to the publication of this book, and I am the happiest I have ever been. I have found and married the love of my life. I have two wonderful stepdaughters, and my wife and I have an amazing daughter of our own! We own a home, travel, take mini-vacations at every opportunity, and are always focused on how we can continue to grow and build together.

Additionally, I have savings and investments, and am in great physical shape. I eat healthier than ever, have a home gym, and actively train in martial arts. One of the most important changes I have made is no longer having a toxic relationship with alcohol! I am free from the burdens, setbacks, and disappointments it brought into my life. It is fascinating how many of these outcomes were once desires that were handwritten in my notebook when we first began mapping out the template ideas for *Tilting The Balance*™.

While there are plenty of other changes I have made, those are some of the more significant ones. If they may seem like a lot to you, know that they did not happen overnight, nor all at once. These were small adjustments done consistently. Changes in my awareness, mindset, feelings, decisions, and overall outlook on life.

With that said, know that when you are attempting to reach your goals, obstacles can, and most likely will, get in the way. Some challenges may be within your control, while others may not. Sometimes the timing is wrong for certain areas of your life, and other times areas do not need as much focus because you are happy where you are at the moment. This is why you cannot be discouraged if you fall short of your goals, as it is bound to happen at some point. No one is perfect, and we will all encounter obstacles in life. The key is to not quit, to keep moving, and if you fall, to get back up and start over. You are not in a race with anyone else! This is for you and your life.

To provide a great example, when COVID-19 happened, which was definitely beyond our influence, it gave me the opportunity to start writing this book. It also substantially dropped my income that year, which ultimately led me to new employment opportunities, new relationships, and stronger friendships. During this time, I was also able to work on another passion of mine: painting. Throughout this project, every experience has helped me to "tilt the balance" in my life, learn new things, discover more about myself, grow in my relationships, and understand what is most important.

Occasionally, we catch ourselves comparing our journeys to others. Thoughts about whether we should be further along by now, or wondering why other people seem so much further ahead, naturally creep in. Our time will come though! We just need to stick with it, keep going at our own pace, and if we need a redo, that is okay, too. I know I have had plenty of those moments in my life, and here we are. I am not even close to who I used to be, and I know that I am not who I am going to be yet either. We are always evolving, and it is up to you whether that change is positive or negative. The best part is, you are your own person, on your own timeline.

You can do this. You can become better in every area of your life if you want to. You can achieve your dreams and find the love you desire. You are special, capable, and amazing. I truly believe in you!

Thank you for reading this book. We hope you enjoyed it, and I deeply pray that your life is always changing for the better.

Stay blessed,

Nicolas A. Houpt

ACKNOWLEDGMENTS

Justin M. Bullock & Nicolas A. Houpt would like to extend a special thank you to the following individuals:

A special thank you to all of you authors, whose work we have collectively mentioned and referred to throughout this book. Without all of your hard work, dedication, and insights, we likely would not have many of the understandings we do today, be the men we are, or had ever made this book a reality for the world.

Thank you, Mr. Gokul Madathil, for all of your hard work and monumental assistance with the creation of this book. Without you, this book would have taken much longer to have been completed, and who knows, it may not have ever been completed at all...

Thank you, Mr. James Chakhtoura, for your amazing graphic design skills creating such a phenomenal book cover, logo, and helping with the book templates.

Thank you, Mr. Richard Dellamorte, for all of your hard work, insight, proofreading, and editing. You have been a tremendous resource for us.

Thank you, Mr. Harvey Brown, for all of your hard work, insight, proofreading, and editing.

Thank you, Ms. Beth Schneider, for all of your hard work, insight, proofreading, and editing.

Thank you, Mrs. Olivia Hale, for all of your assistance with the book templates and photography.

Thank you, Mr. Grayson Marshall, Jr., for all of your positive encouragement, insight, and support.

Thank you, Mr. Brandon Stanko, for all of your professional legal counsel.

Thank you, Mr. Amit Dey, for all of your amazing services aiding us in correctly formatting all of our works.

Ms. Michelle Hill, thank you for all of your wonderful insight and assistance with connecting us with the best resources we needed to complete this book.

And Mr. Thomas Strunk, thank you for your guidance and mentorship.

We sincerely appreciate each of you and could not be more grateful.

–Justin M. Bullock & Nicolas A. Houpt

CO-AUTHOR ACKNOWLEDGMENTS

– Justin M. Bullock

This is a list of individuals who have all had some form of positive and significant impact in my life, outside of the list of those we already mentioned in the shared acknowledgments. I want to thank each of you for all of your guidance, influence, support, love, and friendship. I love and appreciate each and every one of you:

Aaron Caulder • Abe Ahmed • Adam Locklear • Addison Saba • Al Torres • Alex Crews • Alex Kaiser • Allen Williams • Amanda J. Fisher • Andrew "Bud" Orth • Anthony Cincotta • Ashton Wilkins • Austin "Ash" Hamilton • Austin Peltier • Benjamin Hudnall • Benjamin Welter • Blake Whiddon • Bob Kegan • Brendan McClendon • Brendan Winans • Brian Bayne • Brian Bullock • Brian R. Edwards • Bryan J. Welter • Carlos Brisolla • Cassandra Saslona • Charles Caraway • Chelsea Belanger • Chris Lane Jones • Collin Gorey • Conor Albritton • Damon Lee • Dana Brown • Dana Porcelli • Daniel Kim • Daniel Luckett • Daniel McCarthy • Dara Sweatt • David Andrews • David Bayne • David Miller • David Myers • David Tilson • Denise Burroughs • Dennis Boboc • Diane Parkman • Donald Fann • Dylan Lawson • Edith Farmer • Eric Andersen • Ericka Imbrunone • Frank Mattar • Frank Spaulding • Gary Booth, Jr. • Geoff Burt • George Arut • Gina Morrison • Glenn Connelly • Glen Friedman • Glen Riser • Heliana Brown • Hussein Hussein • James F. "J.D" Dukes, Jr. • Jason Amey • Jason Cleary • Jason Parker • Jeff Holyszko • Jeff Kordenbrock • Jeff Lerner • Jeffrey J. Meredith • Jennifer Price • Jerome Crawford • Jesse Dent • Jesse Lane • Jesse Wyatt • Jesus Leon • Jimmy Easterling • Joe Kennedy • Joel Brown • John Dahlke • John Germaine • John Peterson • Jonas Albertie • Jon Hurm • Jordan Dahl • Joseph Janssen • Joshua Warren • Julia Strunk • Kari Hendry • Katherine Hobson • Kathy Ornstein • Katie Kane Kozlowski • Katrina Myers • Kellie J. Long • Kelimae Mills • Kevin Durkin • Kevin Johnson • Kevin Peacon • Konstantin Ryabov • Korissa Kingen • Kris Pederson • Kyndal Ray Edwards • Lauren Wiktorek • Lee Barido • Lenny Jennette • Liann Francisco • Linda Collins • Lorraine Sheridan • Luis Carreja • Mark Kaiser • Marsha Bayne • Martin Goodman • Matthew Tueschel • Melissa Brown • Melissa Cooper • Michael Kingen • Michael Francis I. Labelle • Nancy McEvoy • Nancy Schlefstein • Nancy Trippitelli • Nicolas A. Houpt • Philip Markijohn • Raj Mody • Richard Farmer • Richard Fernandez • Richmond Gard-Chambers • Robert Foote • Robert Lemus • Rodger McDowell • Ronald Raynor • Ronald A. Tremblay • Ryan Beach • Ryan Wegner • Sara M. Simpson • Sean McCarthy • Shane Carreja • Shankar Thayver • Sheena Kennedy • Sheldon Diggs • Sherrie Simpson • Sky Streety • Spencer Wolfe • Steven Wiktorek • Sudha Thayver • Taylor Stafford • Terri D. Collins • Thomas C. Hollister • Tiea Vincent • Timothy Hightower, Jr. • Timothy Hightower, Sr. • Tyler A. Kordenbrock • Warren Cooke • Wendell Charles • Wendy Rigotti • Wil Ingram • Wesley Bey • William Armbrecht • Wyatt Lambeth

A special note of deepest gratitude goes to Thomas Strunk, whose influence has been the most pivotal in shaping my life and this work.

Each of you individually will forever hold a special place in my heart.

With Gratitude,

Justin M. Bullock

CO-AUTHOR ACKNOWLEDGMENTS

– Nicolas A. Houpt

This is a list of the people in my life that, if not for them, I would not be where or who I am today:

Alex Kaiser • Andrew Servey • Boden Carter • Casey McNeil • Chad Anfinson • Dan Mulvihill • Ed Leto • Ernie and Joann Cohen • Ethan Nicholas • Hans Boehm • J.J. Barber • Jami Kelly • Jim Webb • John Moses • Jordan and Jessica Heaps • Justin M. Bullock • Laura and Amy Kaiser • Matt Ehrhart • Matthew Terrill • Michael Rhoads • Mike Anderson • Mitch Elmore • Omar Rodriguez • Peter Louies • Randy Justice • Robert Wood • Ryan Abney • Steve Wiktorek • Thomas Houpt • Toni Marinelli

Special acknowledgments to my Dad, Terry Houpt, for always being there no matter what and raising me to be the man I am. My Step Mom, Kelly, for always seeing my true potential and pushing me to be a better version of myself.

To my Mom, Thea Justice, for having the courage to bring me into this world at such a young age and helping me through the hardest times of my life.

To my Mamaw and Pap, Tom and Becky Houpt, for helping raise me, your help and support, and the lessons and memories in life that I continue to use and cherish to this day.

And to my wife, Olivia, for being there helping me throughout the process of writing this book, all of your love and continued support, and for keeping me grounded.

I love you all,

Nicolas A. Houpt

WORKS CITED

Dispenza, Joe, and Daniel G Amen. *Breaking the Habit of Being Yourself: How to Lose Your Mind and Create a New One*. Carlsbad, Calif., Hay House, 2015.

Olson, Jeff, and John David Mann. *The Slight Edge*. Plano, Texas, Success, 2013.
Abrahamson, Alan. Michael Phelps: *No Limits the Will to Succeed*. New York, Scholastic, 2008.

Bowman, Bob, and Charles Butler. T*he Golden Rules*. St. Martin's Press, 17 May 2016.
"Michael Phelps - Think Small to Accomplish Big Things." *www.youtube.com*, www.youtube.com/watch?v=Y8ZZS0qrVNw.

Byrne, Rhonda. *The Secret: The 10th Anniversary Edition*. New York, Ny, Atria Books; Hillsboro, Or, 2016.

Gardner, Sarah and Albee, Dave. *Study focuses on strategies for achieving goals, resolutions* (2015). Press Releases. 266. https://scholar.dominican.edu/news-releases/266.

Oettingen, Gabriele, et al. "Self-Regulation of Goal-Setting: Turning Free Fantasies about the Future into Binding Goals." *Journal of Personality and Social Psychology*, vol. 80, no. 5, 2001, pp. 736–53, doi:https://doi.org/10.1037/0022-3514.80.5.736.

Clark, C. J., Liu, B. S., Winegard, B. M., & Ditto, P. H. (2019). Tribalism Is Human Nature. *Current Directions in Psychological Science*, 28(6), 587–592. https://doi.org/10.1177/0963721419862289

Mehta, R., and R. Zhu. "Blue or Red? Exploring the Effect of Color on Cognitive Task Performances." *Science*, vol. 323, no. 5918, 27 Feb. 2009, pp. 1226–1229, https://doi.org/10.1126/science.1169144. Accessed 24 Mar. 2019.

Wintle, Walter D. *"Thinking."* Unity, by Unity Tract Society, Unity School of Christianity, 1905 edition.

Singer, Michael A. *Living Untethered: Beyond the Human Predicament*. Oakland, Ca, New Harbinger Publications, 2022.

Szegedy-Maszak M. "Mysteries of the Mind." US News World Rep. 2005 Feb 28;138(7):52-4, 57-8, 60-1. PMID: 15765847.

Duhigg, Charles. *The Power of Habit: Why We Do What We Do in Life and Business*. New York, Random House, 2012.

Izard, Carroll E. "Emotion Theory and Research: Highlights, Unanswered Questions, and Emerging Issues." *Annual Review of Psychology*, vol. 60, no. 1, Jan. 2009, pp. 1–25, www.ncbi.nlm.nih.gov/pmc/articles/PMC2723854/, https://doi.org/10.1146/annurev.psych.60.110707.163539.

Cascio, Christopher N., et al. "Self-Affirmation Activates Brain Systems Associated with Self-Related Processing and Reward and Is Reinforced by Future Orientation." *Social Cognitive and Affective Neuroscience*, vol. 11, no. 4, 5 Nov. 2015, pp. 621–629, www.ncbi.nlm.nih.gov/pmc/articles/PMC4814782/, https://doi.org/10.1093/scan/nsv136.

"SellingPower.com." *Www.sellingpower.com*, www.sellingpower.com/2010/02/02/3723/team-up-with-mary-lou-retton. Accessed 22 Feb. 2023.

Bennett, Roy T. *The Light in the Heart: Inspirational Thoughts for Living Your Best Life*. United States, Roy T. Bennett, 2020.

Dimberg, Ulf, et al. "Unconscious Facial Reactions to Emotional Facial Expressions." *Psychological Science*, vol. 11, no. 1, Jan. 2000, pp. 86–89, https://doi.org/10.1111/1467-9280.00221.

Cooper, Ella A., et al. "You Turn Me Cold: Evidence for Temperature Contagion." PLoS ONE, vol. 9, no. 12, 31 Dec. 2014, p. e116126, https://doi.org/10.1371/journal.pone.0116126.

Be Inspired. "*You Will Never Be Lazy Again* | Jim Kwik." YouTube, 21 Mar. 2019, www.youtube.com/watch?v=REeROakzwfU. Accessed 14 July 2020.

Wayne, Corey. How to Be a 3% Man, Winning the Heart of the Woman of Your Dreams. Lulu Press, Inc, 20 June 2017.

National Institute of Mental Health. "Mental Illness." *National Institute of Mental Health*, Jan. 2022, www.nimh.nih.gov/health/statistics/mental-illness.

CDC. "About Mental Health." *Centers for Disease Control and Prevention*, CDC, 28 June 2021, www.cdc.gov/mentalhealth/learn/index.htm.

National Alliance on Mental Illness. "Mental Health by the Numbers." Nami.org, National Alliance on Mental Illness, June 2022, www.nami.org/mhstats.

Umberson, Debra, and Jennifer Karas Montez. "Social Relationships and Health: A Flashpoint for Health Policy." *Journal of Health and Social Behavior*, vol. 51, no. 1, Mar. 2010, pp. 54–66, www.ncbi.nlm.nih.gov/pmc/articles/PMC3150158/, https://doi.org/10.1177/0022146510383501.

Teo, Alan R., et al. "Social Relationships and Depression: Ten-Year Follow-up from a Nationally Representative Study." *PLoS ONE*, vol. 8, no. 4, 30 Apr. 2013, p. e62396, www.ncbi.nlm.nih.gov/pmc/articles/PMC3640036/, https://doi.org/10.1371/journal.pone.0062396.

"Tony Robbins: The Secret to Living Is Giving | Big Think." *www.youtube.com*, www.youtube.com/watch?v=T7Etxod0a0A. Accessed 22 Feb. 2023. PAGE 146

Robbins, Anthony. *Awaken the Giant Within*. London, Pocket, 2004.

Hall, Manly P. Ten Basic Rules for Better Living. Philosophical Research Society, 1 July 1996.

"National Study by FINRA Foundation Finds U.S. Adults' Financial Capability Has Generally Grown despite Pandemic Disruption | FINRA.org." *www.finra.org*, www.finra.org/media-center/newsreleases/2022/national-study-finra-foundation-finds-us-adults-financial-capability. Accessed 22 Feb. 2023.

"66% of Americans Are Worried They'll Run out of Money in Retirement – Here Are 7 Tips to Make Sure That Doesn't Happen." *GOBankingRates*, 28 Sept. 2022, www.gobankingrates.com/retirement/planning/tips-make-sure-dont-run-out-money-retirement/. Accessed 22 Feb. 2023.

Maxwell, John C. [@TheJohnCMaxwell]. "Remember, a budget is telling your money where to go instead of wondering where it went." Twitter, 11 February 2016, https://twitter.com/thejohncmaxwell/status/697827645896192000.

Daly, Lyle. "How Frugal Are You? Compare Your Monthly Expenses to the Average." *The Ascent*, 22 Feb. 2022, www.fool.com/the-ascent/research/average-monthly-expenses/.

Doran, G.T. (1981). "There's a S.M.A.R.T. way to write management's goals and objectives." Management Review. 70(11): 35-36.

Patricia Pulliam Phillips, and American. *ASTD Handbook for Measuring and Evaluating Training*. Alexandria, Va, American Society For Training & Development, 2010.

"That's What Friends Are For." *ScienceDaily*, 2017, www.sciencedaily.com/releases/2017/04/170420113921.htm.

Lally, Phillippa, et al. "How Are Habits Formed: Modelling Habit Formation in the Real World." *European Journal of Social Psychology*, vol. 40, no. 6, 16 July 2010, pp. 998–1009, citeseerx.ist.psu.edu/viewdoc/download?doi=10.1.1.695.830&rep=rep1&type=pdf, https://doi.org/10.1002/ejsp.674.

Hermann Ebbinghaus. *Memory: A Contribution to Experimental Psychology*. New York: Dover, 1885.

"Landing on Everest: Didier Delsalle Recalls His Record Flight." 2017. Vertical Mag. November 15, 2017. https://verticalmag.com/features/landing-everest-didier-delsalle-recalls-record-flight/.

Palahniuk, Chuck. *Fight Club*. New York: W. W. Norton & Company, 1996.

Clear, James. *Atomic Habits: An Easy & Proven Way to Build Good Habits & Break Bad Ones*. New York, Avery, 2018.

Sinek, Simon. *Start with Why: How Great Leaders Inspire Everyone to Take Action*. New York, Portfolio, 2009.

Pressfield, Steven. *The War of Art: Break Through the Blocks and Win Your Inner Creative Battles*. New York, Black Irish Entertainment LLC, 2002.

Dalio, Ray. Principles: Life and Work. New York, Simon & Schuster, 2017.

Robbins, Tony. *"How to Turn Setbacks into Successes."* TonyRobbins.com, Robbins Research International, 13 Feb. 2023, www.tonyrobbins.com/blog/how-to-turn-setbacks-into-successes